CHANGING CONCEPTS OF RETIREMENT

KU-207-663

STUDIES IN EDUCATIONAL GERONTOLOGY

General Editors

Frank Glendenning
Honorary Senior Research Fellow, Centre for Social Gerontology,
Keele University and Department of Continuing Education,
Lancaster University

David Battersby
Professor and Dean of the Faculty of Health Studies, Charles Sturt
University, New South Wales

Also in this series:

Good Practice in the Education and Training of Older Adults
Alexandra Withnall and Keith Percy (1994)

Learning and Cognition in Later Life
edited by Frank Glendenning and Ian Stuart-Hamilton (1995)

Changing Concepts of Retirement: Educational Implications
edited by Joanna Walker (1996)

Reminiscence and the Empowerment of Older People
Joanna Bornat (forthcoming, 1997)

Teaching and Learning in Later Life: A Critical Perspective
David Battersby and Frank Glendenning (forthcoming, 1997)

Changing Concepts of Retirement

Educational Implications

edited by

JOANNA WALKER

© Joanna Walker 1996

All rights reserved. No part of this publication may be reproduced, stored in a retrieval system, or transmitted in any form or by any means, electronic, mechanical, photocopying, recording or otherwise, without the prior permission of the publisher.

Published by
Arena
Ashgate Publishing Limited
Gower House
Croft Road
Aldershot
Hants GU11 3HR
England

Ashgate Publishing Company
Old Post Road
Brookfield
Vermont 05036
USA

British Library Cataloguing in Publication Data
A CIP catalogue record for this book is available from the British Library.

Library of Congress Catalog Card Number: 96-83833

ISBN 1 85742 259 7

Typeset by
    Michele Bailey
    Pre-Retirement Association
    Guildford

Printed and bound in Great Britain by
Hartnolls Limited, Bodmin, Cornwall

Contents

Figures and tables

Contributors

Lorna Andrew is a counsellor, trainer and supervisor of counsellors who has worked specifically with young people, with couples and with retired and pre-retired clients and groups. She was until recently a lecturer in counselling in the Department of Educational Studies at the University of Surrey. She has now retired and is learning to put theory into practice.

Anthony Chiva is an educator at Surrey University, Department of Educational Studies and the Pre-Retirement Association of Great Britain and Northern Ireland working in course and project development. He has published work on managing change, living skills and self-development.

Mary Davies is currently Director of the Pre-Retirement Association of Great Britain and Northern Ireland, and has been involved in education as a teacher, lecturer and producer of educational materials. She has been a researcher and consultant in the areas of health and sexuality.

Mike Hepworth is Reader in Sociology at the University of Aberdeen. His main research interest currently is the analysis of the part played by visual and literary images of ageing in the construction of the ageing experience. He has been a member of the Executive Committee of Age Concern Scotland and a founder member of the Centre for the Study of Adult Life at the University of Teesside.

David James is a psychologist and educationalist with interests and publications in learning in later life. He is currently President of the Pre-Retirement Association of Great Britain and Northern Ireland and Chairman of the Association for Educational Gerontology and his local Age Concern and Pre-retirement groups.

Peter Jarvis is Professor of Continuing Education and currently Head of Department of Educational Studies at the University of Surrey. He has written numerous books on adult and continuing education, and made contributions to the field of educational gerontology, and enjoys an international reputation as a teacher and writer.

Joanna Walker is a member of the Department of Educational Studies, University of Surrey, and Resources Information Manager for the Pre-Retirement Association, with an interest and publications in the education of older adults, and in developing pre-retirement education within an educational gerontological context. She has been a founder member of the Association for Educational Gerontology.

Series editors' preface

This is the third volume of the series *Studies in Educational Gerontology*. Importantly, it addresses the way in which concepts of retirement have changed. Our understanding of the meaning of 'retirement' has changed markedly in the last thirty years. This has affected our perception of the necessary models of pre-retirement education and senior adult education and practice. The book sets out a radical review of the meaning of learning for adults who are 'retired' or in later life. This is a mature reflection on the findings of the education for older adults movement, during the last twenty years.

From the study of pre-retirement and retirement education, the book moves on to consider the management of change after the cessation of full-time paid work. It discusses adaptation and survival after change, the relation between learning and change and development and personal growth. The context of learning in an ageing society raises issues also about the ageing self, the implications of being and learning on what is, historically, the eve of the millennium, and the specific educational needs of those in later life who are disadvanted.

We warmly welcome this important addition to the series. It charts out new territory in relation to education in later life and makes a firm contribution in our view to the development of educational gerontology as an emerging field of study.

Frank Glendenning and David Battersby
Series Editors
December 1995

Editor's preface

The idea for this book was first generated in a public house in Maynooth, County Kildare, under the influence of a Council of Europe conference on older and unemployed adults that was taking place nearby.

The need identified in such congenial surroundings was, surprisingly perhaps, for a text that made explicit the links between education and gerontology, and the academic base for pre-retirement education. The challenge that this task involved was the synthesis of material that I hope will be thought-provoking to both educators and gerontologists.

I trust that it will also make sense to the growing band of practitioners and academics who call themselves educational gerontologists, but for whom the literature has been somewhat disparate. Frank Glendenning and David Battersby's series, of which this is one part will, of course, help establish a core of current thinking.

The book is arranged in three main sections. The *first* lays foundations, looking first at gerontologically derived concepts and then educational ones and, lastly, at their combined study.

The *second* section then views the whole field from an individual differences (or micro) perspective. It enquires about individual and subjective factors in older adults' capacity to engage in learning; and how these affect participation and outcomes.

The *third* section focuses on the social factor in the equation, the wider contexts in which learning, ageing and experiencing take place. This volume makes no detailed reference to either the practice of older adult learning, or examples concerning it. There is also no discussion of older people's capabilities for learning. Although relevant to the theme of this volume, both of these topics are the subjects of fuller examination by other titles in this series.

The nature of the interaction of individuals with their social environment is a key question in social science, and the construction of the ageing experience for both individuals and for society has never been so relevant.

Joanna Walker
December 1995

Acknowledgements

I would like to thank the contributors to the text, who have been willing to share their expertise for the purposes of this book. They have also contributed in other ways. David James and Peter Jarvis have encouraged me in my academic work with Surrey University for over a decade. Mary Davies and Tony Chiva have given support and friendship as colleagues in the Pre-Retirement Association. Mike Hepworth and Lorna Andrew, with whom I have worked in teaching and on conference programmes, have skills as communicators of their own special knowledge and understanding that I have appreciated.

The Association for Educational Gerontology has also been a source of input and inspiration to the thinking that this book represents, and I congratulate it for the influence and support it has provided for over ten years now to educational gerontologists in many work settings.

Frank Glendenning has been a colleague and a mentor and has given generously of his time and experience in guiding this particular project.

Michele Bailey has worked unstintingly and with great skill to produce a typeset work from probably the last manuscript to be handwritten.

My immediate and wider family have offered both support and interest for which I am grateful.

This book is dedicated to Brian Walker, 1924-1995.

PART I
Foundations

1 Concepts of retirement in historical perspective

Joanna Walker

Retirement is essentially a social institution implying transition out of another formally recognised social role, that of paid employment. Unlike ageing, it cannot have a solely private or individual aspect to its existence, since it can only occur as a result of engaging in social relationships and arrangements. Although ageing can and does have social dimensions (which in turn create both social and private meanings) ageing is an intrinsic characteristic of living beings. In contrast, retirement, whilst it may well form a part of our contemporary experience of ageing, can only be socially created and understood and is, as such, more subject to change in response to social forces.

Retirement is very much a creation of Western industrial society, where relationship to the means of production is a primary organising concept in most domains of human study. In practical terms, retirement is a social outcome of work being organised outside of and divorced from the household, and has been developed in order to facilitate the continuity of effective workforces.

Ironically, because this is the first time in the history of the world so that many people have lived so long, the concept of retirement has grown during the course of the century to embrace various social meanings and features of later life, simply as greater numbers survive beyond the social act of withdrawal from employment (which is the original and commonsense meaning of retirement). The term retirement now refers not only to the event of leaving employment but also to life after paid work, and new concepts have arisen in order to generate knowledge and understanding of this new situation, which could no longer be simply characterised by a negative state - an absence of employment.

Most notably there has arisen the idea of a 'third age' - that following the first age of childhood and schooling, the second age of employment and homebuilding, and preceding the fourth age of decline and dependency. The nature of such a third age has been a focus for much study and activity in recent years. Its power, for the purpose of this book, is as an organising concept that has brought together the potentially disparate debates about work-ending and ageing. The increasing ambiguity of the former, and the greater understanding of the latter (through the development of gerontology), have conspired to put retirement onto both academic and public agenda as never before.

In discussing concepts of retirement we need an awareness that although ageing is a factor in their composition, these are not concepts of ageing per se. Ideas about ageing, and their more organised expression in theories of ageing, can be found in the domains of biology and psychology (for example), and in applied fields of study and practice such as medicine and education, and a range of supportive and therapeutic interventions.

Concepts of retirement focus more specifically on the change in the social relationships that characterise withdrawal from employment-related roles. Such roles can be quite broadly defined - almost anything that makes a social contribution, whether paid or unpaid since, arguably, most activity can be seen as having a socio-economic impact at some level. Concepts of retirement, then, chiefly feature notions of change, role, social engagement.

In the following review of retirement concepts the history of understanding in this area will be traced and described under these broad groups:-

Retirement as
1. an event, a period, a social institution
2. the third age, a new name for retirement?
3. a life-stage within a life-course perspective
4. productive ageing
5. a subject of industrial gerontology

1. The event, the period, the social institution

This section relates the story of retirement as it most obviously appears and can be evidenced in social policy. Stanley Parker has offered historical accounts (Parker 1982, 1987) that chart the isolated beginnings of 'age-related work exit' in the early nineteenth century through to its growth during the twentieth century into a practice of almost universal acceptance.

Even in its early stages, retirement was often linked with receipt of a pension. Cessation of employment was rewarded or even induced by payments which would relieve the worker of the need to continue in employment, most usually due to the special demands of the job (e.g. pension for police with 25 years service, introduced in 1890) or in recognition that a lifetime of low wages extended the need to work well beyond an age of efficiency (eg. elementary school teachers given retirement and pensions at 60 in 1892).

Parker (1987) comments that these increasingly numerous early occupational pension arrangements were fixing retirement at 60 or 65, reflecting the belief and the experience that this was the age beyond which most people could no longer physically work. In the early twentieth century, however, and once public policy had become involved through the introduction of a state pension in 1908, the timing of the age-related exit ceased to simply recognise the situation of older workers, but could become a proactive tool of economic and social policy.

Parker's analysis is that philanthropic concern for the aged poor was less influential in shaping retirement than the demand for greater workforce productivity in the face of overseas competition at the end of the nineteenth century. Such concerns did however ally usefully with Trades Union worries about potential redundancy of older workers who could not meet new productivity demands. The spread of occupational arrangements for retirement and pensions, and for a state scheme as back-up, were part of the response to these pressures, and resulted in the creation of a socially recognised and accepted category of non-worker - that of retiree or pensioner.

Parker (1987) goes on to describe that, once established as a policy tool, the timing and eligibility for state recognised retirement have been adjusted during the twentieth century to meet various socio-economic demands. The history of retirement this century has also been conceptualised and charted by Phillipson (1982, 1987, 1993) as the emergence of a social institution, taking on a social character of its own, full of complexities and paradoxes unintended by its instigators. The 'event' of retirement, the act of withdrawal, has become a larger entity, bound up with the fate in society of older people as a class. Thus Parker (1987) concludes:

> A survey of the history of retirement in Britain thus points inescapably to the conclusion that older people - at least working class older people - have generally been treated as reserve of labour. In periods of slump, for example, they may be drawn out of the labour market more quickly than other groups (particularly unskilled and semi-skilled older workers); in periods of labour shortage, the justification for retiring and becoming a 'non-productive consumer' may be questioned as part of a campaign to call back or retain people in the labour force.

> It is difficult to escape the conclusion that in all these successive periods of first rare retirement, then discouraged retirement and currently

5

encouraged retirement the elderly have been thought of, and indeed used, primarily as a reserve labour force. In the latter period, however, part of the encouragement to retire has been to present it as a social and political right to be guaranteed independently of shifts in the economic climate. The marginal economic position of the elderly continues to be tacitly accepted. (Parker, 1987 pp.80).

In similar vein Phillipson (1982) observes that in the 1930s and 1980s the requirement on older workers to contribute economically through employment was downplayed because of mass unemployment, whilst their ability and eligibility to retire was stressed. In the 1950s, by contrast, they were 'passengers', threatening society's economic standing if not productively employed.

Phillipson notes the double irony of this latter attitude, in that retirement (withdrawal from employment) became a qualifying condition for receipt of state retirement pension (National Insurance Act 1946) just as the social status of retirement in public opinion had become acceptable. However the more influential trend was the policy-related fear of the demographic shift to an ageing population. The post-war period thus found itself stressing the advantages of employing older workers in order to decrease the acceptability of retirement and the so-called 'idleness' of old age.

Since the 1980s, when mass unemployment turned the tables yet again, setting in train the biggest trend towards 'early retirement' across the industrialised world, the complexity of the picture has increased. The pressures of increasing numbers of older workers and their increasing health status are in conflict with major social trends in the way paid work is organised and distributed.

Technological change and major reductions in semi- and unskilled jobs in traditional industries have made a nonsense of 'normal' retirement which, in historical terms, had not been with us that long. The boom period between the unemployment of the 1980s and 1990s again illustrated the effect of older workers being wooed for their skills and experience. Now in the second half of this decade public expectations about retirement are in a state of confusion.

Those convinced in the late 1980s by the arguments about older workers' value to the workforce (including older workers themselves) are left in the 1990s warning about the skills and experience shortage that will result when an upturn is finally achieved (but at which point the over fifties will be largely no longer employed by anyone). Whilst many take this warning seriously, and some employers strive towards good practice regarding their older workers, the economic reality of later life redundancy and unemployment continues unabated. De facto, the event of retirement often arrives unannounced and ten years earlier than the 'baby-boomer' generation expected.

The unravelling of the welfare state is set to return retirement to its early twentieth century character. Public pensions will only support those defined as in need, with private savings and insurance provision (whether brokered through employers or not) reverting to centre stage as sources of income in later life. The event of retirement then returns once more to the private domain of individual economic circumstance, though subject to such social or fiscal pressure as governments exert on financial institutions.

The reality of this situation for many people can be seen already in the promulgation of 'portfolio' employment (self-managed careers, involving a mixture of short-term or consultancy contracts punctuated by periods of unemployment, retraining, family care, etc). There is pressure on government to fill the policy gap that has opened up concerning 'discouraged' workers in their fifties who in reality will never work again.

The response is being framed within the context of the latest episode in the story of retirement. In the 1990s, then, we see the swing away from the encouraged (or 'early') retirement of the 1980s towards discouraged or delayed retirement. This is presumably because delaying payment of state pensions will save more money than increasing unemployment claims, since a large proportion of those 50 years and over will not claim through 'discouragement' or ineligibility.

The prevailing economic philosophy of self-help and independence will, as ever, put more choice into the hands of some groups in society and reduce it for others. The choices involved in the event of retirement will be no exception to this rule.

2. The third age - a new name for retirement?

As we have seen, the expectations people may have about being in or out of employment at different ages (in response to social, economic and technical change) constitute a confusing picture of 'retirement'. Once could be de facto retired, having experienced an age-related work exit such as redundancy at 50, yet not be eligible for state or private pension support. One could be engaging in a mixture of short-term part-time employment and for-expenses-paid voluntary work at 67, whilst drawing both state and private pensions. Do these two circumstances have anything in common that could contribute to a concept of retirement?

It has been proposed that retirement has also come to refer to the period of life that follows full-time employment as well as the event of leaving work, or means of exit from the labour market. This gives scope for a concept of retirement that relies on something other than the presence or absence of paid work which, as in

7

the examples above, can lead to a narrow and unworkable definition. The 'third age' has moved into popular understanding during the 1970s and 80s as a concept that embraces the ambiguities of age-related unemployment, and in doing so offers an understanding of retirement (as a period of life) that is less employment centred. It describes a stage of life in which the social imperative to be employed is weakened, to be replaced by a more self-directed style, characterised by diversity of activity restricted only by personal resources. The third age has been defined as an era of 'personal fulfilment', following the second age of independenc, maturity, responsibility, earning and saving, and preceding the fourth age of final dependence, decreptitude and death. (Laslett, 1989, p. 4)

Thus characterised, is the 'third age' more of a candidate for a concept of ageing than of retirement? It does of course also function well in that capacity but, arguably, it says so much about the changes in social engagement, roles and expectations of life in this period (usually defined as 50-75 years) that it also stands as a useful contemporary model of retirement.

If asked to account for the emergence of a 'third age', most commentators would cite some or all of the following:

- more people living into later life, with better health
- a better standard of living for retired people, compared with the past, if not with other groups in society
- average age of retirement having decreased, retirement now sometimes chosen rather than mandatory
- recognition of, if not adequate provision for, need to continue a range of activities in retirement
- identification of a third-age 'lifestyle', encouraged by consumerist interests
- growth of self-awareness among third agers of common causes? (eg. older people's rights to services, fighting ageism, conflict of interests with younger groups etc.)

One of the criticisms of the third age concept is that it is a cultural, class-laden category, since the lifestyle implied is only open to persons of middle class and middle income and above. However, as Parker (1987) notes, retirement (as an event) also started out as the preserve of the privileged a century of so ago. Superannuated positions were by definition middle-class, secure, well-paid. Working class people reaching state pension age became old age pensioners rather than 'retired', since this latter term implied the possession of an occupational pension and/or significant savings. Today all occupational levels commonly lay claim to the term 'retiree', implying both withdrawal from employment and financial entitlement of some kind for most.

8

Will the third age develop a similarly broad acceptance as a way of understanding and presenting retirement as a period of life? Can the idea of third age contain the great diversity of personal material resources that are available to people in this age group?

Kohli and Rein (1991), remind us that the ambiguous term of retirement can refer to an event, a process, a role or status, or a phase of life. They add that it can also be indexed by several other criteria such as objective indicators of work, income or pension receipt or by subjective ones based on self-assessment. They note that authors and researchers often use combinations of these factors as retirement definitions with the resulting conceptual weakness of "highly divergent populations of retirees" and also allowing for "the possibility of transitions back out of retirement".

Because they feel that counter-transitions are a conceptual nonsense, they adopt a somewhat stricter definition of retirement as "the event of entering into the public old-age pension scheme, or the phase of life beginning at that point."

Would the adoption of a 'third age', which might or might not begin at an agreed point, provide such researchers with a neater concept, which accepts "highly divergent populations of retirees", since ambiguity of social and economic status does seem to be the primary characteristic of this age group? In order to explain the gap between workforce exit, and entry to public old-age pension schemes (retirement), Kohli and Rein provide the notions of pathways (institutionalised routes) and personal routes (individually worked-out sources of support). Allowing the third age to function as a concept of retirement does enable the path/exit taking, the route finding and the entry into new forms of social engagement all to be handled as experiences with features in common.

In noting the rise of the term 'Third age', Laslett (1989) attributes its popularity to the perennial need for a term to describe older people that is not already tarnished, by which he refers to ageist stereotyping. Although now passed into a more general understanding and acceptance, Laslett's definition of the third age is somewhat sharper. The boundaries between the ages are not related to birthdays or even clusters of years around particular chronological ages. So although the life career is seen as possessing four modules, these should not be regarded as stretches of years, but identified by the quality of life experienced. Thus a third age may be lived alongside a second age if personal achievement is being experienced at the same time as other life tasks are being carried out associated with second age. In this case, "no passage from one to the other need occur, for an individual with these characteristics is doing his/her own thing from maturity until the final end". (p. 4)

There is great advantage in labelling as 'third age' the character of the life experience as opposed to an inevitable period of time (whenever this is deemed

9

to occur). It takes the fear out of fourth age, since this can be of minimal length, and may encourage society to stop confusing this last era with the general nature of later life. Thus third age is a better notion than 'third quarter of life', attached to the 50+ age group, because this latter implies anything up to a twenty-five year period of decline.

Reflecting on the implications of his rearranging the socially-accepted 'facts' about later life, Laslett notes that "redividing the life course, and giving its most important component a somewhat novel name, may not go very far" (p. 6) His greater purpose is to present the intellectual and human challenges of this unprecedented period of human history where most members (of advanced societies) have a good chance of a full life-span.

> For the age constitution of our society has been transformed, quite suddenly and without our realising (it). In addition, the institutions and instruments which have been created to meet the *problem* of ageing are in no position to provide us with a policy for the great majority of people who present no problem at all. We need a new outlook . . .(and) a new set of institutions. (p. 2)

Since the third age according to Laslett's formulation is not age or even age-group related, its relationship to the social institution of work stands open to negotiation. There should be no need for withdrawal if personal fulfilment is being experienced. This position, radical in its implications, does indeed challenge the 'institutionalised' views we have tended to take about the life course, and its expectations about later life and retirement.

3. Retirement as a life-stage, within a life-course perspective

Two propositions underpin this approach to understanding retirement, according to Kohli and Rein, 1991. First that recent studies of youth, middle and later life all point to the necessity of contextualising the study of any age group within a life-course framework; second that the life course is itself socially constructed which, in contemporary Western society, means that it is highly institutionalised, they argue.

The institutionalisation of retirement as a life-stage was traced as a broad historical process when considering retirement as 'event, period and social institution', but in this section, retirement in life course perspective focuses on the presence and absence of gainful work across differing age cohorts, and across the

10

life span.

The life course has emerged as an important concept describing a pattern of social rules which order various key dimensions of life such as family and career, as well as the age-related gradings required by state systems eg. education, social security. This 'bureaucratization' of life is also identified by Parker (1980) as a context for understanding retirement.

Kohli and Rein (1991) propose that the recognition of the life course has arisen (again, in the West) because: a reliable life-span with material security is now more commonly experienced than previously; life phases and transitions between them have become more standardised through participation in public social systems (e.g. education, health, mass markets); personal biographical development has also become the subject of social and cultural expectations (through consumerism, popular media, etc.).

Within gerontology, the life course perspective has gained in importance as both explanation and context for many areas of study. Ageing is indeed lifelong and not short-hand for describing older age. Applied more particularly to retirement however, rather than the broader study of ageing in later life, does the Kohli Rein proposition (p. 20) that "the modern life course consists of a standardisation of life events keyed to chronological age" stand up to the ambiguity of retirement in the 1990s?

The argument for the standardisation of the life course runs thus: By the 1960s contemporary retirement had established a tripartite expectation of 'normal' biography as preparation for work, active work and inactive retirement. This last section had a uniform entry stage, co-terminous with entry into public pension systems, and synonymous with an understanding of 'old age'.

This situation had come about because the organisation of production had changed from being based on household economies, to being based on the recruitment of free labour, rather than family members. This in turn required the matching of the availability of workers to the needs of producers ie. the synchronising of organisational timetables with the life courses of individuals. The result, it is argued, was a normalised biography produced by the institutions of work and welfare, giving rise to public systems of education and retirement that standardised childhood, adolescence, adulthood and old age - and all in response to structural changes in economic production.

So strong were these economic forces, it is suggested, that the importance of chronological age categories grew in a period of modernity even when other *ascriptive* criteria (e.g. age, gender) were decreasing in favour of *achievement* criteria. Social order has indeed become less based on ascribed status and locality, and more on engagement with life-course programmes. But this social process, essentially one of individualisation, seems simply to replace the predictability of

11

status derived from a particular group or locality with the predictable progress of individuals through both time and the social structure.

Has the arrival of 'early exit' significantly disrupted this life-course analysis of retirement as a social institution characterised by chronological predictability? Even if its social timing changes, is it not nonetheless predictable? The modern life course, certainly up until the 1960s, was divided into preparation, active work and retirement (synonymous with old age). The challenge to this comes firstly in terms of timing in the form of the 'new life-time budgets' (p. 21). These have been brought about since 1960 by earlier average retirement ages (a drop of about five years) and a corresponding (two-year) rise of life expectancy at age 60, producing a significant lengthening of retirement life.

Does a second challenge, to the triparte nature of the well-established modern life course come closer to dislodging its dominance? Kohli & Rein (1991) maintain that although early exit has allowed the transition to retirement to become "longer and fuzzier" it is still a transition between two very distinct states.

> Most people at age 55 and below still work, and most people at age 65 and beyond do not; most people below 55 gain most of their income from work, and most people beyond 65 gain most from retirement pensions. Thus there is little evidence that the education-work-retirement lockstep is breaking up. (Kohli & Rein, p. 23).

Moreover, it is argued, this lockstep has become more prevalent by spreading to other strata of society, most notably to women, who have been 'incorporated into this life-course regime' (p. 21) through labour force participation. So, they argue, the experience of work life may have become shorter but it has also become more pervasive in society.

The timing of retirement, then, may be earlier, less predictable, more a matter of personal agenda, even subject to 'counter transition' back into the work force. It is nonetheless still a significant and recognisable transition that most people experience in some form, thus supporting the notion of retirement as a life-course event. The more significant challenge may come from whether the changes of the last thirty years amount to a 'de-institutionalisation' of the second half of life, thus halting the process of chronological standardisation that life-course analysts predict.

For it is not only the transitional phase (the period of years over which most people will experience retirement, and referred to earlier as between 55 and 65 years of age) that has become individualised and less predictable, it is the whole period of retirement life itself. This has changed

> from a restricted left-over period, to be lived through without much ambition, to a significant new period of life to be filled by new projects *for which there are as yet few valid cultural guidelines.*" (p. 23, my emphasis).

The issue of predictability is perhaps now focusing less on the exit (from work) stage of retirement and more on the problem on re-entry. Retirement to what? What are the life-course goals, expectations and timings, now that retirement starts in our fifties and goes on until the nineties? Moreover, as the range of activities and experience open up, the security of public pensions and social support is decreasing, along with the legitimation of a non-earning (or non-self supporting) status in society. Thus the relationship of retirement and productivity stands open to renegotiation, where until recently these had been mutually exclusive.

Those who embrace the idea of retirement as the third age will find in this painfully-reached conclusion no surprise. It is in many ways an obvious observation that retirement has become more than one life stage. However the economist's perspective that seems to drive much life-course analysis inevitably focuses on the distribution of work and relationships to the means of production across the life-span. Retirement has been concerned with the largely technical issues of withdrawal from productivity and the maintenance of social security systems. Gerontologists studying the complex human issues bound up with ageing, being economically independent or dependent, following and finishing careers, negotiating new social identities etc. have benefitted from the contributions of socio-economists. The forces that shape the contexts for retirement are now better understood.

As suggested initially in this chapter, retirement (unlike ageing) is a social concept that has little meaning except in relation to paid work, so that the technicalities of retirement timing and prevalence have been increasingly appreciated for their social significance. Not surprisingly these have not turned out to be straightforward matters, as the history of research in this area has shown. This will be discussed in further detail under the section on industrial gerontology in this chapter.

4. Retirement as productive ageing

The relatively recent emphasis on making the case that retirement can be a productive period of life has brought together a number of strands of thinking.

Gerontologists have for some time been building the case that later life is not characterised by dependency, ill health and inactivity, these being the experience of the minority rather than the majority of 'normally' ageing individuals. One logical outcome of the striving to demonstrate not only the capabilities but the positive assets associated with maturity is the current enthusiasm for later life 'productivity', using the term with its economic meaning more or less intact. Debates have accordingly arisen about the extent and nature of productive activity in retirement (what counts as productive and why), and whether viewing later life as having productive capacity is a good thing or not.

Another strand contributing to the popularity of productivity comes from those whose concern has been to find, within modern culture, roles and activities appropriate to retirees. Work has been rediscovered as an essential aspect of human life that meets needs for stimulus, status and satisfaction (Glanz and Neikrug, 1994). The discovery has been not so much that such needs still exist in later life, but that there seem to be no adequate alternatives to work for meeting them. There are many obvious reasons why substitutes have not been found, which need little rehearsal:- people of any age will resist unemployment if possible, since it reduces social contact and opportunity for work satisfaction; the protestant work ethic is alive and well and operating upon motivation at the individual level encouraged by current social and economic climates; the possibility of avoiding or reversing retirement would appeal to those for whom ageing is an unresolved issue; the cultural need to find role and meaning in later life activity can be solved by the easily recognised value of a job.

These advantages of work in later life are now being echoed, though somewhat faintly against the general din of recession, by those workers and employers who have discovered in practice what researchers have been claiming, namely:- that older workers are a vital part of the work force, and employing them makes good business sense; older workers demonstrate maturity, loyalty and customers like them; they are trainable, longer-serving and suffer less absence from work. Beyond paid work, older people's contribution to the grey economy, to volunteering, and to family support of other workers is incalculable.

In order to examine the value of 'productive ageing' as an understanding of retirement, the concept requires clarification, since it is handled with varying meanings within the literature. For some authors, productive ageing simply requires an acknowledgement that retirement is a useful and potentially positive period for both individuals and society. This outlook has parallels with the prevailing philosophy of traditional pre-retirement education which enjoins people to seek a fulfilling and useful life which can be deemed 'successful' retirement. This view is a logical extension of the general position adopted by

14

gerontologists in affirming later life as a normal rather than an abnormal state. Butler (1985) writes in his overview chapter in one of the first texts in this area

It is not that longevity has extended the period of incapacity;rather it is our inability to adjust our expectations and environmentsso as to encourage and allow elderly people to exercise their capacities.Unless we can begin to perceive older people as productive, their lives will be at risk. They will be seen as a burden (Butler and Gleason, 1985, p. 3).

Attempting to be more specific, Glanz and Neikrug (1994) propose what productive ageing is and what it is not (p. 24). They suggest that it is 'part of the world of work', but only meaningful work. It is not 'toil'; 'tedious labor' or undertaken out of necessity. Older people doing this kind of work are not ageing productively, but making ends meet because they form a sub-group of the poor. Glanz and Neikrug note 'The relief of poverty in old age is the proper responsibility of social policy and not the goal of productive aging' (p. 24). We shall return to this point later.

So productive ageing is not labour, or occupational therapy; rather it is the activities of those seeking to express creativity and pursue meaning. This obviously raises a host of difficulties about how such activities can be defined, compared or even encouraged. Activities such as letter writing, socialising, or private mental exertion may well be meaningful but are they productive in the general sense implied by this quasi-economic approach?

Bass et al (1993) are clear that such essentially private pursuits are valuable and fulfilling rather than productive, for which definition activities would need to be capable of being counted, or assigned some economic value. It may also involve accomplishment, or contribution to the quality of life. In other words, productivity involves recognisable outcomes in the public rather than private domain, thus emphasising the role older people can play in society. In contrast 'successful ageing', at the more inclusive end of the spectrum of what counts as productive, places more emphasis on individual capabilities and performance, (mental and/ or physical).

Productive aging is any activity by an older individual that produces goods or services, or develops the capacity to produce them, whether they are to be paid for or not . . excluding activities of a personal enrichment nature (Bass, Caro and Chen, 1993, p. 6).

So participation, education and training that 'enhance capacity' would be productive, but not education for personal growth. This corollary has raised difficulties, as can be imagined. Educational gerontologists' experience of continuing education with older learners usually leads them to expect a fluidity of approaches to, and uses of, learning opportunities in later life.

Beyond these specific debates, the general thrust of the productive ageing approach to retirement is that it acknowledges a swing away from retirement as a roleless role and, significantly, away from retirement as leisure. The contemporary pattern of the non-participation of older people in the work force has been a product of particular social and economic forces, namely the strength of economies to not only support large numbers via pensions and savings, but also to do without older people in the labour force. In changing circumstances where these conditions may no longer hold, or in countries where these developments have not yet become universal experience, the existence of retirement as a choice between leisure and meaningful activity becomes less relevant. The critics of productive ageing as a model for retirement are most mindful of these very situations, where the ability and/or desire to be productive is translated into the requirement to be so. They argue that the gathering opponents of welfare and social security programmes could use the potential of productive ageing as a justification for cuts in public funding support of older people in order to decrease the burden of non-productive elders on the state.

In addition to the important political implications of the double-edged quality of productive ageing, as just described, the other serious criticism of the concept relates to issues of meaning and control for the individual. Productive ageing is assumed to focus on the outcome not the intention of the older person's activity, on the product not the process. Thus the meaning and the success of the activity is defined by an externally imposed value set, rather than by what the individual deems worthy of serious pursuit and investment of energy.

Moody (1993) takes up this challenge, by distinquishing between adopting productive ageing as (i) a regulative ideal for later life, and (ii) a framework for public policy, and by considering what is gained and lost in each case. On the productive outcome vs. the intention question, he illustrates by refering to politicial behaviour, contrasting the thoughtless voter, whose activity nonetheless generates an outcome with the citizen who may hold a deeper more abiding interest in political matters.

Surely, he says, it is

> reasonable to think of this broader altruistic motivation as a form of social productivity and, therefore, as an ingredient of productive ageing (p. 31).

Moody goes on to ennumerate other forms of active citizenship, such as participation in cultural life as well as the economy which could be described as productive. But he identifies one major drawback in pressing the case for productive ageing, which lies in productivity's associated value of efficiency: If we insist on the productivity of the old, we put the last stage of life on the same level as the other stages, setting up a competition in which older people are eventually doomed to be the losers. In doing so, instrumental values (the power to accomplish, create, etc) are favoured above other meanings which society, including older people, may wish to ascribe to later life.

In public policy terms, then, Moody, along with others, sees the virtue in productive ageing as an idea as long as it remains an option, a matter of opportunity not coercion. In order to promote this stance from being 'attractive but inadequate', he makes some policy suggestions that might help policy makers take productive ageing more seriously. These include: tackling age discrimination and mandatory retirement ages; empowering and (re-)training older people for productive roles; inducements to employers / communities to offer paid and voluntary jobs.

Moody identifies the traps of social control, and the extended bureaucratisation of the life course, whilst stressing the facilitative even liberating potential of productive ageing. Such an analysis enables comparison to be made between the productive ageing debate with its fairly sharp issues, currently being drawn out, and the fairly well-accepted concept of the third age, with its softer boundaries. Perhaps we had not fully understood the political and social challenges that the proponents of the third age laid before us until the harsher climates of the 1990s gave us productive ageing.

5. Retirement as research subject - industrial gerontology

Retirement as an area of academic study has been touched on, through reference to both theory and research findings, within the preceding sections. In this last section, the concept of retirement as it has been mapped, described and explained by research will emerge. Retirement as a research discovery has been largely claimed by social science, and particularly by sociologists, although psychologists have contributed significantly, as have the broader humanities and applied sciences.

For this section's purpose, focus is on an area described by American sociologists of the 1970s as industrial gerontology, (Sheppard, 1970) and said to be a new field of applied research and service, using a multi-disciplinary approach to employment issues and processes and consequences of ageing. It was to discuss, for example, issues of employment and retirement of older workers, the nature of work, training and job design, transition to retirement, criteria and preparation for retirement and retirement resources.

The multi-disciplinary nature of such research is clear from such a list, and it appears that gerontological literature in general is relatively rich in contributions that span one or more disciplines, regardless of the disciplinary background of researchers and authors. Since the same can be said of education, then both industrial and educational gerontology (see chapter 3) are well placed to study the complexities of retirement, and give it a shape that will aid our understanding of people's experience, and its social significance.

In the first section of this chapter, the story of retirement was traced relying much on Parker's analysis of retirement, characterised as an event, a period and a social institution. This basic and powerful paradigm has inspired others to elaborate, to test, to redefine. Phillipson (1993) gives four examples of differing research understandings which have been generated concerning retirement. It has been portrayed, he suggests, as a mechanism for facilitating individuals' withdrawal from social life; as an institution to redistribute work from older to younger workers; as an aspect of wider movement towards a leisure society; as a significant mechanism by which dependency in later life is socially constructed.

Moreover, Phillipson notes, these explanations are themselves generated within the dominant value system of society whereby, for example, there is a pre-disposition to see retirement as a problem because work is valued so highly. He traces a history of retirement as a research construct, which can be summarised under a number of themes:

Historical perspectives: Historical scholarship continues to provide an increasingly sophisticated understanding of how later life and its social and economic consequences were viewed and dealt with at different periods, leading inevitably to complex social policy-oriented debates in more recent times.

Paradoxical perspectives: As retirement was becoming a mass experience of the twentieth century, a tension arose between the 'triumph of retirement' as a growing social institution, and the less than universal view that it was a positive development. Post war social policy included periods of active discouragement of retirement in order to redress manpower shortages. At the same period (circa 1950-1970) the dominant research themes were seeing retirement work-loss as a personal crisis with problematic social and psychological impacts.

Retirement as a social and individual problem was a powerful version of events that still has echoes today. Studies from many disciplines appeared to show negative effects (eg. on well-being, adjustment etc.) Some of these findings Phillipson attributes to the methodological differences of cross-sectional research which could not reliably distinguish between causes and effects of retirement. Meanwhile the experience of retirement was growing in terms of numbers

18

reaching retirement age, the decreasing incidence of post-retirement paid work, and the numbers receiving state and occupational pensions.

Complex perspectives: Researchers responded to this paradoxical picture by acknowledging and pursuing greater complexity in their project designs and data interpretation, and Phillipson (1990) describes the variety of lines of enquiry that followed. In particular he notes that, within a general shift which challenged the view that retirement necessarily created problems, there were new theoretical understandings. Role theory and the disengagement thesis gave way to analyses based on the stratification and social construction of later life. Most significantly, a major focal shift took place whereby researchers asked less about individuals adjusting to retirement and investigated more the social factors that defined and influenced retirement choices and circumstances.

Contemporary perspectives: From the largely social perspective that now dominates (as just described), it is possible to focus again on some of the questions that drove earlier researchers. Now that the socio-economic map of how contemporary retirement is structured and likely to be encountered by particular groups at particular times, the effects of its interaction with individuals and their life courses can be re-examined. Understanding the causes and incidence of early retirement, for instance, enables us to ask about its impact on the individual without framing the enquiry or our analyses entirely in terms of how someone adjusts psychologically, or what training might assist. We can even take the view that early retirement can cause problems, without leaving the solution in individuals' hands alone.

Setting retirement in a social frame allows for greater differentiation in experience to be understood. Phillipson's (1991) identification through empirical research of five pathways to early retirement enables a potentially better response to the differing situations represented. Thus 'early retirement' is not of itself a problem, any more than retirement was in the 1950s. It is an outcome common to a number of sets of social forces and individual characteristics, which may or may not require similar action being taken. This distinction is particularly important when seeking to draw out the educational implications of the changing understandings of retirement, especially where educational provision is seen as instrumental in some way in alleviating social problems.

What other research themes currently inform how contemporary retirement is understood? The growth of gerontology has added another significant factor to the analysis for those who investigate stratifications within society - that of age, alongside class, gender and ethnicity. The dimension of differentiating by age has brought with it many new concepts such as age cohorts, 'convoys', life-course transitions and role-allocation timings, age-related development and identity (re)construction. Researchers are led increasingly to question the nature and meaning of age and ageing, and within industrial gerontology these questions have acquired an urgency and sharpness brought on by the pace of socio-economic change.

This has been a brief tour of the academic endeavour that has been defined as industrial gerontology, which cannot do justice to the literature, greater in the United States than the United Kingdom, but both illustrating the methodological and theoretical difficulties in commenting on such a complex area of human activity. Phillipson (1990) concludes that the current debate on retirement research is predominantly within a *continuity-discontinuity perspective*.

Whereas discontinuity had been the prevailing assumption, suggesting that retirement produced dislocating effects common to everyone, research now illustrates that retirement is shaped as much by continuities as discontinuities. The dominant assumption is now of the relationship between retirement and other life-course phases, which accounts for a picture of great variation in retirement experience because it reflects life-long inequalities and differences. Unlike the disconnected experience portrayed by disengagement and role theory, retirement is one more resolution of an individual's social position, sustainable into old age if advantageous, or susceptible to further loss if disadvantageous, because of the relatively low social status of old age, Phillipson argues. He concedes, however, that whilst class position translated into retirement may form a real life context of resources and restraints, it does not explain everything.

The issues of meaning and identity that are highlighted by retirement as the 'third age' and 'productive ageing' are also acknowledged by gerontologists of the political economy school, of whom Phillipson and Walker are examples. Retired people may feel their class position to be ambiguous, once separated from wage labour and may respond instead to different priorities and circumstances. The existence of two sets of social relationships may therefore be a feature that differentiates retirement as a phase. One is the set of life conditions carried forward, the other the set acquired on joining a general group (Phillipson, 1990) of lower socio-economic status. Walker (1986) suggests more research is needed on the former set (continuities) and others are keen to add further dimensions to life course stratification, such as the mediating effect of cohorts in historical time, the construction of life 'careers' or strands, the progress of social identity through biographical analysis and life review.

Notwithstanding the outcomes of all such research, Phillipson identifies some future trends and research directions:

- the continuing loss of older workers from, and their marginalisation within, the labour market
- the increasing recognition and acceptance of retirement as a social institution,

part of the predictable life course.

- the increasing polarisation of resources available to retirees, some able to continue a middle-aged lifestyle into retirement, many restrained by former disadvantage compounded by age.
- social and political attitudes changing from encouraged to discouraged retirement, to reduce the pensions burden and increase flexibility (upwards) in retirement age.
- high levels of financial and social insecurity on the part of older workers, both in and out of employment, who continue to be called upon as cheap reserve labour.
- continued state ambivalence to retirement as a social institution, and thus continued tension concerning the potentiality of retirement life vs. the legitimacy of occupying the position 'retiree'.

2 Models of retirement and educational practice

Joanna Walker

The various ways in which retirement has been understood have been explored in Chapter 1 with reference to gerontological concepts and debates. The task of this chapter is to start to make the links between educational concepts and practices and the changing experience of, and ideas about, retirement. This linkage will be made initially in the broadest sense, by tracing the obvious educational implications of retirement in terms of the concepts already identified, and then proceeding to more concrete issues. The questions are immediately raised as to why educational implications need be identified in the first place, and what might be relevant educational practice, involving what purposes and parties.

Education is usually understood to involve change in knowledge and understanding, attitude and behaviour, skills and personal development. It is distinguished from incidental learning resulting from daily life or the process of maturation, (Peterson, 1990) although in adults its efficacy is related to drawing on the learner's state of experience and understanding to date. A key purpose might be that

> education offers a means of better comprehending the complexity of life and relating oneself more adequately to that complexity (p. 2).

Examples of more concrete purposes might be to learn new skills, to develop an existing interest, to improve one's social or psychological relationships, to gain recognition of one's expertise, or to solve particular problems. If such elements go towards meeting the 'complexity of life' then they surely have relevance to the anticipation and experience of retirement, the complexities of which have already been sketched, and to which relevant educational challenges can be attached. Such challenges, it should be noted, relate both to the individual and to wider society, but whose best interests may not necessarily be consonant.

23

Making initial links

An enhanced understanding is the main educational value of *retirement as event, period and social institution*. It raises the consciousness that retirement is not only a date, albeit a socially significant one, but has a duration for which some agenda may be required. Most significantly, retirement has a social character and image with which the individual will need to interact, raising issues of identity, activity, power and purpose. Battersby (1990) states his belief that a major purpose of education concerning retirement should be to assist older adults to develop an understanding of how the society in which they live impacts on older people and creates variations in their lifestyles and culture.

The third age as a new identity for retirement also implies a fresh understanding of the nature and potential of this period of life. Furthermore, and springing from the appreciation of the post-work phase as gain rather than loss, the demands on education will go beyond preparing and coping and towards self-actualisation, involving creativity and personal development. Education in service of the third age could offer such objectives as empowerment and emancipation, for being as well as doing, for creating meaning as well as measurable outcomes, to which Moody (1993) would have it aspire, for example. Here we encounter education for citizenship, for cultural transmission to younger generations, volunteer and leadership roles, as well as an array of personal achievements, (Laslett, 1989) To pursue Laslett's 'fresh map of life' metaphor, education to prepare for one's third age passage (or even make sense of the journey if already started) might reasonably include an understanding of the likely terrain, the arts and skills of travelling safely and successfully, and some purpose in the journey if not the details of the route or destination.

The *life course concept of retirement as a normative stage*, with its varying interpretations of social vs. individual control, would most naturally invoke the current emphasis on lifelong or continuing education. Education for retirement would then form a part of an existing pattern of educational participation, taking place throughout the life course and involving training and retraining; education for interest, personal growth or leisure; for specific roles whether work, family or community oriented, paid or unpaid; to help deal with particular difficulties or challenges. As with the original gerontological concept, the educational approach would emphasise continuities, and the building-up of experience and competences throughout and across differing life-stage demands.

Productive ageing, whilst demanding similar things of education as the third age and life course versions of retirement, is more focused in its educational implications. With an emphasis on producing outcomes of social and, if possible, economic value the most appropriate educational form would be training.

Preparation for productive retirement could involve updating knowledge and skills for continued employment or volunteer roles, retraining for new endeavours building on past experience or untapped potential. Continuity and development are again the themes, stressing the 'normal' nature of retirement life, rather than its diminished or disadvantaged status. In order to promote this understanding among others, particular skills such as assertiveness, communication, campaigning etc. would also represent relevant training needs. Educational demands specifically excluded by productive ageing would include learning for personal development, for its 'own sake' or interest, or other unproductive purposes.

Retirement as a research construct, subject of industrial gerontology, has no intrinsic educational implication although the educational needs associated with retirement can be observed and assessed empirically. The literature on older adults and learning, whilst not large, identifies various themes, eg: learning capacity, motivation, participation, outcomes, environments, types of provision, appropriate methodologies, curriculum issues etc. Some of these will be explored more fully in Chapter 4.

The education for older adults movement has been pursuing these linkages for some years and, in the form of the Association for Educational Gerontology, since 1985. It has been concerned to enable professional reflection on research, practice, and the education and training issues for personnel involved with older adults. Within this frame of interest have been those who have a particular involvement in handling and presenting ideas about retirement to middle aged and older people, and also to those who employ mature adults or provide them with services. In Britain, the USA and continental Europe this area of interest and practice has been known as preparation for retirement (PFR) or pre-retirement education (PRE).

More specific links, the case of retirement education

The understandings of retirement that retirement education personnel possess will obviously influence the nature of the preparation and learning that they will be able to facilitate for mature adults contemplating later life. It can be argued that, until a more systematic effort to train and improve the practice of such pre-retirement educators was begun in the 1980s, concepts of retirement were neither explored, nor perceived as relating to practice. The contemporary prevailing ideas about retirement had been taken as the given situation to which retirees must adapt.

Models of retirement, then, were few and for the most part unconsciously operated by the educator and retiree alike. However, as has been described earlier,

25

the original understandings of this new mass phenomenon of retirement began to evolve more complex theories and models, and a greater variety became available. But retirement education practitioners were not usually gerontologists, neither were they working in contexts where relevant literature, or the inducement to seek it out and assess it, were available. There were, of course, a small and influential band of academics and industrialists who did engage in theoretical as well as practical interests in retirement education.

The two major intellectual inputs to the fledgling pre-retirement movement were gerontology and adult education. Reflecting on its history, pre-retirement educators have tended to conclude that the movement quickly became more involved in developing provision to meet the discovered need, to the detriment of developing theoretical understandings to inform practice. As intimated above, these did not re-emerge until research into the quality of practice (in the later 1970s, early 1980s) led to interest and supporting resources being put into training and professional development from the 1980s onwards.

Reflecting on practice usually leads to revisiting purposes and philosophies that are bound up in provision. Whilst some interest in education for and about retirement had been part of the education for older adults movement over a similar time scale (discernable in 1950s and 60s and gathering pace in 1970s and 80s), practice in the field of pre-retirement education had become largely divorced. Theoretical stirrings had begun however, and challenges to the prevailing model of retirement offered to retirees were mounted, as well as to the teaching and learning styles of contemporary (pre)retirement courses.

Specifically, research (Phillipson and Strang, 1983; Coleman, 1992) had criticised (inter alia) the instructional, didactic nature of courses as being inappropriate for adult learners. A related difficulty was, of course, the unexamined model of retirement that existed in the mind of course providers. If retirement was a discontinuous devalued status, liable to cause problems to individuals dealing with the loss, and which situation required acceptance rather than negotiation, then an instructional / training mode may not be inappropriate. It may be that it has not been until relatively recently, when the whole understanding of retirement has been opened up and come more to public notice, that links between models of retirement and educational practice concerning it have been made.

There follows an analysis of models of retirement that have been identified along with their related theoretical constructs and educational practices. They are arranged roughly, though not strictly, in developmental order. Commentary will be made following the table.

Table 2.1
Models of retirement

Model of Retirement	Theoretical / research background (Gerontological)	Related educational objectives	Issues / content for retirement programme	Teaching / learning style
Banking	Structural functionalism, Role discontinuity, (Disengagement Theory)	• prevent crisis of loss, minimise psychological and social stress • Facilitate acceptance of and adjustment to new status • maintain morale	Relevant information for future use in new life deposited. Appropriate activities and attitudes suggested.	Instructional Didactic Pedagogic 'Expert' - led
Successful Retirement	Activity Theory, Substitution theory	• prevent decline by promoting 'substitute' roles for work loss. • encourage positive, optimistic outlook	Information and suggestions as above, but more aggressively positive, encouraging action as well as acceptance.	as above
Life-Phase Transition 'Life Switch'	The institutionalised life-course, role allocation according to life course timings, socialisation to role	• identify and accept change • refocus on new phase with appropriate activity	Significance of life change and transition, reference to past experience. Discussion of attitudes and behavioural choices in life-context. Information and suggestions as above.	Mixture of styles encouraged, didactic and discursive. Peer group and personal experience as well as expert-led.
Transition Process, 'Coping with change'	Life span developmental psychology, Psychology of adjustment and adaptation, social construction of self	• identify and understand transition and change • refer to and value personal experience • increase sense of personal agency within life context	Implementation of decision making model for management of change and future life planning. Issues as per group need and negotiation.	Highly discursive and interactive. Andragogic. Facilitative leadership. Negotiable agenda.

Table 2.1
continued

Model of Retirement	Theoretical / research background (Gerontological)	Related educational objectives	Issues / content for retirement programme	Teaching / learning style
Variations on Transition / Life Planning models (i) Social stress model (ii) Coping with Uncertainty (iii) Comfort Zones	Life span developmental psychology, Psychology of adjustment and adaptation, social construction of self	Similar to above:- ● understand transition process ● reduce and control potential stress ● take appropriate control through life planning.	Cognitive and affective work as above	Generally androgogic and facilitative as above, with varying degrees of democratic participation.
Lifelong Management of Self (Growth and Change) various models that apply to adults generally.	Lifespan developmental psychology (adult development) Theories of Personality	Understand psycho-social processes that shape the self-concept throughout life, and in relation to life-change.	Review past and present self in order to manage change and plan future.	Small group, interactive style best for learners to appreciate the potential of these models for growth and change.
Life Strands	Life course perspectives (non-institutionalised). Role continuities. Social construction of self and status maintenance.	● understand life continuities and careers ● identify areas of control in life context	Life review Life planning	Andragogical, facilitative. Experientially-based.

Table 2.1
continued

Model of Retirement	Theoretical / research background (Gerontological)	Related educational objectives	Issues / content for retirement programme	Teaching / learning style
Third Age (of fulfilment)	Life course (non-institutionalised) Life span development	• understand qualitative difference of 'third age' • respond to gain vs. cope with loss • engender personal development • increase sense of self	Life planning including self actualisation. Valuing of creativity and aspiration, for being as well as doing.	Andragogic / Gerogogic? Could be mixture of interactive (peer support) or didactic, as long as inspirational.
Productive Ageing (non-retirement)	Biomedical (postponement of ageing) and any theory / findings supporting life-long capacity	• to understand continuity of work / productive roles • to recognise rights to resources and opportunities • to prepare / train for future roles.	Career development. Skills updating. Assertiveness training Achievement oriented	Training style, could be didadic and / or group work based. Instrumental
Counselling model	Humanistic and Lifespan Psychology. Psychogeriatrics (mental health in old age). Sociology of deviance and social control.	educational/therapeutic objects to •(re)learn adaptive patterns of thought, feelings, behaviours. • understand self in relation to 'normal' age-related development and change management.	Problems areas identified. Support and development through counselling or other strategies - Self management and life planning skills	Highly interactive (one-to-one / couple / small group) Client centred or problem-centred
Rite de Passage	Symbolic inter-actionism Social anthropology	• to facilitate transition to new status by marking role exit with a social ritual.	Content of little relevance. Act of participation more important than learning outcomes	Not important as long as culturally significant.

29

Commentary on models of retirement analysis

The models of retirement which form the axis of the above analysis partly reiterate some of the concepts of retirement described in Chapter 1. In this framework, however, they are more numerous than the five categories referred to earlier, because the notion of a model is slightly different. I have used 'concepts' as a grouping together of lines of thought into convenient packages within which commonalities can be found. Models, for this purpose at least, are used to represent and encapsulate more singular ideas or perceptions of retirement. It has been helpful to identify models because, as it has been argued, they are often unconsciously operationalised within educational programmes for and about retirement.

To complete the analysis, linkages have been attempted between the models and their theoretical or research backgrounds (which together constitute the gerontological input) and the educational implications, divided into educational objectives (the purposes for learning about retirement), educational content (the areas of knowledge, skills and attitudes involved in programmes) and the relevant teaching and learning styles or methodologies. Lastly, it should be noted that theoretical and research backgrounds refer to specific theories where these seem particularly relevant, although they may be concerned with ageing rather than retirement per se. Otherwise more general theoretical perspectives are noted, which at least help place the model in a theoretical framework.

The models referred to have been identified from both literature and practice, that is, from abstract as well as practical processes. As such, some are more 'worked out' in educational programmes than others, with a history of reflective practice and development (e.g. Coping with Change). Some are relatively simple ideas, identifiable only because they form powerful assumptions that underlie educational approaches to retirement, but have not had their implications consciously worked through (e.g. Successful Retirement, Life Strands).

Peterson (1990) quotes Moody (1976) as proposing that educators (and other professionals) make one of four pre-suppositions about older people and education:

(i)   *Rejection* of older people as worthless to society, so not worth educating.

(ii)   *a social services* assumption that the disadvantages of later life merit ameliorative action by society, including educational services to occupy people and/or improve their lives.

(iii)   a *participation* rationale that provides education in order to enable older people to continue to play vital and meaningful roles for their own benefit and for that of society.

(iv)   the *self-actualising* potential of later life, which can be facilitated by education which aids the quest for personal growth and achievement, and the integration of lifelong experience and understanding.(Moody, as quoted in Peterson ,1990, p.4-5).

Echoes of the last three of these propositions can be heard in the range of models suggested. There may well be other models operating within the minds of retirement education practitioners, to whom the exercise of critical reflection is recommended. To aid this process practitioners, programme organisers and sponsors (including employers) might also care to own some of the assumptions they see here identified. For instance, the *banking model* is a prime example of an unconscious, uncritical stance adopted by many early programmes, and can still occasionally be observed today. It assumed that preparation is a means of putting something in the bank against the rainy day of retirement, and to soften the blow when it falls. Retirement was implied as being a different (discontinuous) and disadvantaged state, for which an appropriate attitude might be to make the best of it. Positive thinking was required in order to boost morale. Efforts to create reassurance for the future extended on some programmes to learning about local geriatric and paramedical / social services available. The disengagement theory (1961) was still influential in the early days of pre-retirement education, and may have influenced this somewhat strange rite de passage into 'God's waiting room'. Course methods were largely instructional and advisory in nature and a new 'expert' industry was born.

It was probably the discrediting of the disengagement thesis and the entrance, by reaction, of activity theory (1963) and its relation, substitution theory, that gave rise to the particularly pervasive *model of successful retirement*. Success relied upon remaining engaged, particularly in substitutional activity that replaced what paid work had previously supplied. Despite drawing on a contrasting theoretical background, successful retirement was similar to banking in effect and outlook concerning retirees. It was authoritarian, instructional and socialising (to a new role) in its purpose, relating chiefly to externalised values and behaviours, rather than seeking to create understanding or meaning for its participants.

A significant break with this approach can be identified and traced as life-long perspectives in psychology and education begin to succeed in their assault on retirement as discontinuity. However, the life course in this *life phase transition model* is institutionalised, although not entirely contained within watertight compartments. Qualitative differences are ascribed to the different phases in this example from 1986, (cited in Walker, 1992) leading to the notion of transition and the need to manage the change, which might involve adjustment in thinking and feeling as well as behaving. It was also the first published model to show how adult

31

education methodologies and philosophies could be brought to bear, (the need for these in PRE practice had been raised by research in 1982 (Coleman) and 1983 (Phillipson and Strang), op. cit.) alongside other more traditional formats.

However, the life course stages were still perceived as having fairly fixed entrances and exits, requiring adaptation and socialisation to deal with change. A specific programme example entitled 'Life Switch' seems to exemplify this model. The shadow of potential retirement crisis still lurked because the 'switch' could be quite sudden.

Phase 1

▼

First major transition

Duration: a quarter of life?
Including: full-time school for all; further, higher, technical, professional education for some.
Focus: EDUCATION/employment/leisure

Phase 2

▼

Second major transition

Duration: half of life?
Including: employment in some form for some or all of the period, of social and economic importance.
Focus: education/EMPLOYMENT/leisure

Phase 3

Duration: a quarter of life?
Including: self-directed activities and roles, as circumstances and resources allow.
Focus: education/employment/LEISURE

Figure 2.1 Life phase transitions model
Source: Lumbard et al. (1986) cited in Walker (1992, p. 18)

The fuller development of these promising new directions found expression in the *transition process model*, of which 'Coping with Change' is the exemplifying programme. In this approach, acceptance is finally discarded in favour of understanding one's situation, and the model draws more heavily on social-psychological constructs of self, albeit in social contexts (encountered as retirement issues to be identified by course participants). The methodology is unambiguously adult and student-centred, and relies in practice on interactive and group techniques. Expertise is to be found within experience, and exploration of one's future life can be made safely with one's peer group, facilitated by a tutor-guided decision-making model. This contains the elements of *understanding the change, managing the stress, taking stock, considering options, making choices, assessing action*.

The importance of this model has been reflected, in the United Kingdom, by its additional impact on training and professional development. Because 'Coping with Change' has been the subject of action research, field trials and evaluated provision for some years now, it has achieved a recognition that has challenged many aspects of previous practice. Even where the model was not subsequently adopted, it has stimulated many pre-retirement educators to examine their theories, content and methods.

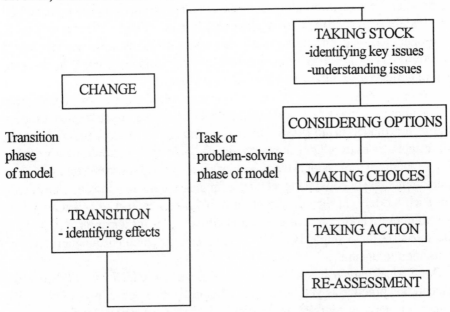

Figure 2.2 Coping with change decision making model
Source: Chiva and Coleman, 1991 p.7.

Some *variants on the transition/life planning model* are worth noting, as they share similar features. They are related to Coping with Change, in that they operate in the same cognitive and affective domains, and focus on a more lengthy or complex transition process than the life-phase model allows. The *Social Stress model* (George, 1980) was a systematic attempt to link notions of loss adaptation to other social and psychological factors in order to build a predictable pattern of retirement transition.

The *Coping with Uncertainty* approach from Canada (Selles, 1995) illustrates a modern pre-occupation with retirement security in the broadest sense, and how to approach translating the present into the future when both states are fundamentally 'uncertain'. *Comfort Zones* is a well-established American concept (with a programme of the same name, see Corbett and Urquhart, 1990) which, like the others cited here, aims to convey an understanding of the retirement transition as a process that can be followed through, and over which control can be influenced. Comfort Zones in particular draws on the metaphor of the retirement process as a journey during which stress can be reduced (and comfort increased) by life planning.

One educational advantage of all of these models, where the process of retirement is the focus, is that programme planning is more flexible and adaptive. The earlier focus on information and advice had to be continuously updated and checked for relevance to different audiences (for, as we know, retirees are highly heterogenous). The process models can speak to many different retirement situations. They are also programmable as face-to-face courses, in distance learning mode or as interactive computerised learning.

Some pre-retirement practitioners having discovered the life-long perspective are beginning to make new additional links between the pre-retirement process and general models of *adult development and change*. They may have encountered these approaches to self development (which could apply to adults of any age) in other spheres of professional practice or from theoretical sources. Some will have more immediate or convincing relevance for pre-retirement purposes than others, but such models (further illustrated in A. Chiva's chapter) offer exciting new possibilities for both practical and theoretical extension in their application to later life. See also, for example, Biggs', S. (1993) reinterpretation of Jungian concepts in relation to ageing.

The *Strands model* has already been cited as one which has no distinctive educational practice as yet, but could be helpfully included in any course which sought to increase retirees' understanding of their situation. Its derivation is clearly life-course in orientation, focusing on continuities in the 'strands' which typify one's experience to date.

A tool is thus provided for an individual to reflect on the his/her 'careers' in various core arenas of life, such as employment, domestic / caring roles, health, learning, financial, leisure, housing, consumption, friendship etc. Retirement is assumed to bring changes, which will vary in their speed, their importance, and in the degree of control that can be exercised. The task is less to manage a predictable social / psychological pattern (as the transition process models imply) but to maintain or reconstruct the strands or threads which one requires for the future. But in common with the process models this implies life review and life planning, which can be facilitated by retirement education.

34

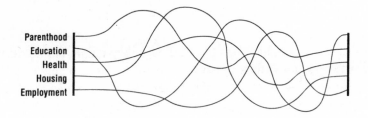

Parenthood
Education
Health
Housing
Employment

Figure 2.3   Life strands model
Source: Allatt, unpublished, cited in Walker (1992, p. 20)

> There is no general change from one state of being to another; a person may be in or out of employment, caring roles or education at any stage. As in a tapestry, therefore, retirement can be as abrupt as a discontinued thread in the employment 'career' or as gradual as a change in the overall pattern or hue (Walker, pp. 20).

The *Third Age model* provides the next significant change of gear in our analysis, following from that represented by the 'continuities' models just described. The key concept of retirement as third age is fulfilment, implying continued development towards a peak, in a period of life previously thought to be characterised by descent or, at the best, keeping level. Indeed so strong is the idea that whenever personal fulfilment is the dominant mode of experience then third age can be said to be taking place at any chronological time in life, even running alongside the second age (Laslett, 1989). This further implies a qualitative difference in retirement living compared with other periods, and for which education must be a key.

First, a great change in consciousness is required to catch the vision of third age fulfilment, as it runs counter to society's version of events. Second, a catalyst may well be required to release creativity suppressed at other life periods; to empower people to demand and develop skills and resources; to build confidence about 'being' as well as 'doing' in a work-centred value system. A very few pre-retirement education and mid-life courses are consciously responding to these learning needs, but more may follow as the implications of the model become better understood. Methods whether interactive or didactic will need to be inspirational and empowering.

Carrying forward the positive status of later life the *Productive Ageing model* stresses the equality of rights to work, training and support to productive roles as enjoyed by younger people. It is, essentially, a non-retirement model, and so the issue of continuity is non-problematic. The educational inputs required would be similar as for third age fulfilment, but much more instrumentally focused, involving, for example, career development, skills extension, including assertiveness and negotiation.

Two further models require mention. Although they do not link to essentially educational implications, they are part of pre-retirement practice, and often function in a quasi-educational mode. First, the *Counselling model*, the theoretical derivation of which lies in applied science and the practice of therapeutic interventions, rather than any gerontological model of retirement as a problem. That retirement is a life stressor and a problem for some is undeniable. Counselling has recently discovered later life as field of interest, and is developing more pro-active approaches as a result of seeing it as more than a period of undifferentiated loss (see Scrutton, 1989). However, coping with loss and change are still strong themes for those who can benefit from counselling. The educational aspects of counselling strategies might be to understand one's perception of, and reaction to, retirement and to (re) learn more adaptive patterns of thought, feeling and behaviour.

The second 'non-educational' model of retirement education is that of *rite de passage* which is essentially social in nature. Some retirement preparation programmes serve this function to a small or even large degree. The model's theoretical roots are back with the life-phase transition / discontinuity school. Its heyday was probably in the 1970s and 80s when employers could still afford to sponsor attendance on programmes where the pre-retirement course, retirement party and parting gift were all part of the same package of social recognition of the past work and status of the retiree.

Jarvis (1989) has commented on the incomplete nature of the 'ritual' view of retirement preparation (which starts, he notes, when the company offers a course). There is a clear element of separation, but no equivalent rite for incorporation into a new role or status. He recommends that educational objectives for courses include a recognition of this situation and the need for people to become their 'own agents' for restructuring themselves a social identity. As long ago as the mid 1970s Tidmarsh lamented the lack of any religious observation that marked the beginning of the major life stage of retirement, as there is for birth and/or church membership, marriage, and death.

Conclusion on 'models'

Surveyed broadly, the models of retirement as interpreted by education seem to show a developmental sweep. They start with approaches that seem to *socialise*, even pacify the individual as (s)he struggles with a qualitative change of status. Key ideas are acceptance and maintaining a positive outlook. Next, the need to acquiesce is overtaken by the need to understand, not only one's position and potentialities, but also the processes that retirement may take one through. Taking advice is replaced by *making decisions,* introducing elements of control and areas of negotiation into the retirement equation. Lastly there begins to emerge a call for *empowerment* that recognises both the 'being' and 'doing' of retirement living, and demands opportunities and resources to fuel to its achievements.

However, we are still dealing mainly in the realms of ideas as we trace from socialisation to decision making, to empowerment. How does this progression match with real life? The socio-economic context of retirement (including the two current major trends of structural change, i.e., in society's demographic profile and in the labour market) has altered in almost every respect since retirement and education first began to make connections. Perhaps the early models dispensing advice and employer largesse could afford to be narrower, since their audience was almost entirely male, white and middle class.

Then, retirement was the unknown for which outside expertise was required. Later we knew, due to the growth of unemployment as well as retirement, that retirement was not so different from other periods of life and change, for which personal experience was available. Later still, when pension and career planning became more the responsibility of the worker him/herself, the imperative to plan on a longer and broader front began to emerge. Moreover, since life in the labour market was now as uncertain as the prospects held out by retirement, the call for greater power of agency in retirement is being heard at a time of general disempowerment for workers. What is there to be lost that has not already been lost?

Marshall (1993) in a masterly summary of social models of ageing identifies groupings of conceptual approaches to retirement, providing another perspective on the models mapped out above. One group focuses on how age-related roles and statuses are *allocated* by the social system giving rise to age-stratification models. The interactions of age with factors such as occupation, educational attainment, cohort effects and historical events are studied.

A second set moves from accepting age-related grading of social positions to emphasising the *social construction* of age gradings, with the admission that at the level of individual experience, life courses contain many anomalies and unpredictabilities. This is the location of the debate as to whether the modern trend for early retirement has untied it from being a normative age-related life course event / transition.

Third, Marshall groups together models which employ more social-psychological elements, to discuss, for example, the impacts of *personality* throughout the life course, implying a progressive elaboration of initial personality differences. Individuals are seen as meeting developmental challenges and adapting to new settings with long term adaptational consequences. Notions of *role socialisation* are also placed in this group since the focus is the interplay between individual and social forces. Marshall notes that socialisation models have

> something of an archaic flavour but in fact they persist in some important current theorizing (p. 16).

A last group brings together models which have *negotiation* as a common theme, including notions of life course careers; life-narratives constructed with reference to a 'convoy of associates'; life planning as future subjective career or 'expected life history', which is the individual's catalogue of future events with a timetable and probability estimate for their occurrence (p. 17).

The ageing self is a powerful concept in this last group, which Marshall defines as the theory a person builds up concerning his/her interactions in the world. Ageing is therefore a beneficial factor, increasing the number of 'tests' to the theory, creating greater stability, continuity and familiarity with many roles. The past can be invoked as evidence of success, edited or enhanced by memory, or even consigned to secrecy where necessary. Negotiation is a central feature because the individual will work strategically to maintain continuity, and to incorporate change into prior history with minimum disruption.

In concluding this chapter on models of retirement and educational practice, Marshall may have the last word as he states his preference for models that credit the ageing person with a greater sense of agency, a capacity for action and a perception of the self as competent. These are ideas that educational practitioners can work with to great effect regarding retirement, especially when complemented by consciousness-raising objectives to enable retirees to appreciate the social forces that contextualise their experience. To paraphrase George (1990), the (ageing) self is an initiator as well as product of social inter-reaction; both protagonist and reactor. The self mediates the impact of social structure on individual outcomes, but also determines behaviour that changes social structure.

3 Educational gerontology: The study of retirement and education

Joanna Walker

As outlined earlier, in Chapter 1, the two knowledge bases from which the interplay between retirement and education can be studied are gerontology and adult education. Five conceptual approaches and some particular models of retirement were outlined, forming a broad gerontological scene into which educational thinking was drawn in Chapter 2, and particular reference made to the educational practice of learning about retirement.

In the last of three scene-setting chapters, the means will be outlined by which we can transfer to the other weight of the dumbbell, that is to educational concepts and practices. This intellectual 'bridge' emerged as a field of study initiated mostly but not exclusively by educationists. In considering of the strengths as well as the challenges of this relatively young academic area, the foundations to the two further sections of the book will have been laid vis, *perspectives on learning* (the province of education) and *contexts for learning* (the province of gerontology).

Educational gerontology was described by Glendenning and Battersby (1993) as meaning

> all that has to do with the practice of education with older adults: its philosophy, its content, its methodology, its evaluation, the training of its tutors and organisers, with special attention being paid to the very considerable amount of education for older adults which operates within a self-help mode (p. viii).

Thornton (1992) defines educational gerontology as encompassing

> all of the educational endeavours associated with the study of aging and being aged designed to meet the learning needs of older people, of the general public, and of workers in the field (p. 416).

Encapsulated in this latter statement are the elements of a debate which has evolved in the last twenty years in North America about the differing audiences and forms of study and practice involved in educational gerontology. Since the task of this chapter is to offer a broad state-of-the-art position the particulars of this debate will not be rehearsed, but readers wishing to pursue the history of the field of study could refer to accounts in Withnall and Percy (1994), Weiland (1995), and to articles which constituted early discussion of educational gerontology's components and scope (Peterson, 1976, 1980, 1983, 1985; Glendenning, 1989, 1990; Glendenning and Percy, 1990; Battersby, 1990; Thornton, op. cit.).

Stating his aspiration of progressing the discussion of older adults' learning, Weiland (1995) explores the need for new forms and frameworks of inquiry, 'beyond demographic justifications, pre-occupation with the problem of participation, and the search for adult instructional principles and techniques indifferent to subject matter (e.g. 'andragogy')' (p. 607).

If somewhat harsh on the adult educators whose concern for older people's learning initiated the field of study, Weiland challenges us to rethink gerontological applications in education and to seek the better integration of gerontological ideas into educational gerontology (p. 608).

The rationale for his stance lies in what he regards as the bipartite nature of educational gerontology - both for and about ageing people. This might be a great strength because it encompasses the *principles of teaching and learning of any subject to/by older adults* as well as the *instructional form of the sciences of gerontology*. In this way

> educational gerontology presents continuities between the interests of those dedicated to older adult learning, and those dedicated to gerontology itself *where it bears directly on education and where it does not* (p. 593, my emphasis).

However, this needs to be reviewed against Glendenning's opinion over the last decade that a distinction must be drawn between educational gerontology (all that has to do with the education of older adults) and gerontological education (the teaching of gerontology at all levels to professionals, para-professionals, volunteers and the general public) (Glendenning, 1985, 1989, 1990, 1994).

The field of study would therefore be incomplete without the theory and practice of the domain of adult education that refers particularly to older adults, and without attention to scientific and intellectual concerns of gerontology and its sub-fields.

Without wishing to labour the point, Thornton (1992) summarises his understanding thus: *Education* uses resources and procedures to support and guide the learning of knowledge, skills and capabilities which can be applied competently and productively. *Gerontology* studies ageing from the perspective of the social sciences (social gerontology) and the health status (geriatrics) of older people (pp. 416-17).

Core *knowledge bases* for study and practice in educational gerontology are thus provided by social gerontology, geriatrics and educational sciences, and its methodological scope is derived from adult education. Educational gerontology's purpose is to provide methods that will disseminate knowledge and skills, and to change attitudes and consciousness about the ageing processes and the older learner (p. 417).

If, in order to succeed in this purpose, educationalists are required to grapple with the intellectual concerns of gerontologists then, Weiner suggests, they need to appreciate the scientific and epistemological issues that characterise gerontology. These arise chiefly from the interdisciplinary nature of gerontology, which can be a source of conflict as well as collaboration.

Whilst it strives to be more than the sum of its constituent disciplines, gerontology has not yet subordinated the claims of, for example, biology, medicine, psychology, sociology, anthropology to a consolidated agenda of its own for research, for curricula on ageing, for educational provision or social advocacy. This is a fundamental dilemma for any multi-disciplinary field of study, whose history will also reveal changes in relations between cohorts of scholars from differing disciplines, raising differing topics, methods and epistemologies for the generation of new knowledge and understanding. (see also Jarvis, 1990 on the evolution of fields of study).

As has been amply illustrated by the concepts and models of retirement previously discussed, the many forms of gerontological inquiry show both promise and flaw. Adult educators undoubtably need the various understandings of retirement and ageing that gerontologists propose, since learning cannot take place *in vaccuo*, and for older adults in particular the impact of life experience, self-perception, socio-economic status, and other social environmental factors have been found to be important. And if gerontological insights are being incorporated in educational thinking and practice, as the development of educational gerontology would suggest, then their reliability and applicability must be matters of concern.

Further to this is the question as to whether adult education is one of the constituent disciplines that contributes to the field of gerontology; or whether it is rather an affiliated enterprise which benefits from gerontological insights across gerontology's range of domains (i.e. other than education) without exerting

41

much influence on gerontology's overall direction? If the latter, which has arguably been the case so far, then how separate can the two enterprises (adult education and gerontology) remain and still be useful enough to each other to allow the development of educational gerontology?

Interestingly, for the first time in 1994, the British Society of Gerontology included in its annual conference a stream on 'gerontological education'. Informal discussion has re-commenced between the two professional membership organisations, British Society of Gerontology and Association for Educational Gerontology, as to their complementary roles and activities.

A diagram follows that attempts to illustrate the relationships between the fields of study, sub-fields, contributory disciplines and practices discussed in this Chapter.

FIELD OF STUDY & SUB-FIELDS	GERONTOLOGY		EDUCATION
	Human biomedicine	Social gerontology	Education of adults
	Cognitive science	Industrial gerontology	Educational gerontology
CONTRIBUTORY DISCIPLINES (to both major fields of study)	Medicine, biology, sociology, anthropology, psychology, policy stdudies, philosophy, politics, history, literary studies		
PRACTICE	Geriatrics Non-medical therapy Rehabilitation	Policy Social advocacy	Adult Education

Figure 3.1 Knowledge bases for educational gerontology

PART II
Perspectives on learning in mid and later life

4 Older adults and learning: An overview

Joanna Walker

Introduction

In 1981 Coppard observed that where later life is equated with decline and older people are afforded few opportunities to participate in society in productive and creative ways, the objectives of learning throughout life become problematic. When educators have a negative view of ageing, life-long learning becomes a way of simply helping retired people adapt to a bad situation (as we have seen). When educators view retirement life realistically and positively, learning for and during this period takes on a greater all-round social importance, including that of the social engagement for older people.

The purposes Coppard therefore proposed for older adults' learning include: continued personal growth, development of understanding, and confidence to participate in society and to work for change. Benefits thus accrue to both individuals and society. Stating his belief in the feasibility of learning throughout life, the interest of older people in it, and the possibility of resources being mobilised to provide it, Coppard nevertheless recognised that several questions needed resolution before older adults' learning could become more universally available, instead of exceptional and marginal.

Fifteen years on it is interesting to note the continuing pertinence of Coppard's questions:- What help or motivation needs to be provided for older adults to pursue learning (recognising that much informal learning takes place regardless of organisation or sponsorship)? How can participation in learning be improved? Are there 'minority' or special educational needs that can be served? How can educational opportunities for older adults be defended in times of scarce resources? What forms of learning will be most appropriate and effective? What is the relationship between different experiences at various life periods?

Learning and later life

Jarvis (1989) argues that the early development of the mind and a sense of self are themselves *learning* processes based on internalising and memorising experiences of the world. The mature individual therefore comes to possess a learned store of knowledge, skill, attitudes and values that make up his/her universe of meaning which is the basis for understanding future experience. Thus equipped, much of daily living can be enacted without conscious thought, Jarvis suggests, until a situation or an experience occurs that is outside the individual's store of understanding. When such a disjuncture occurs, 'between biography and experience' (p. 164), then conscious learning is required.

Furthermore, it is argued, that since these kinds of uncertainties are unavoidable, human behaviour becomes habitualised, and group norms are established for behaviour as well as for patterns of understanding. At the level of society, bureaucratisation adds a legal framework and law enforcement, organised religion, rules for citizenship etc. But the elaboration of such structures, whilst providing ready-made extensions to the individual's store of understanding for phenomena not yet experienced, also run counter to that other great human urge to explore what is unknown or novel in any situation. Jarvis goes on to argue that these 'potential learning situations' at the disjunctures of experience will stimulate the individual to make one (or more) of a variety of responses in order to transform the new experience into the existing repertoire of knowledge, skills and understanding. But learning will not invariably result from 'potential learning situations' because (i) the challenge to the existing store may not be sufficient, (ii) a 'ready-made' solution may be adopted, (iii) there are several 'non-learning' responses to the challenge to experience as well as the learning ones. These 'non-learning' responses are: to *extend* a presumption out of past experience to cover the new situation; to simply *avoid* the issues and not engage with the challenge because other matters are too distracting, or life is too complex; to *reject* the learning opportunity perhaps because the disjuncture appears too great to master, change has been too rapid, or other threats are perceived.

Whilst acknowledging that learning is a much wider concept than education (which is a process that may be part of learning) educators take close interest in what factors might turn these 'non-learning' responses into learning ones. It also follows from Jarvis's arguments that although effective *adult* learning in particular is closely related to previous experience, experience itself need not result in learning taking place (See also Jarvis and James in this volume).

In applying this analysis of experience and learning to mature adults it can be seen that whilst learning can be a life-long process, the experience which at an earlier stage helped to structure a person's understanding may or may not continue to aid the learning process. The logic of the argument suggests that older age, and thus greater experience, may require increasingly less learning. However, there are two reasons (at least) why this does not follow. First, people may have restricted their learning responses (as described above) at any stage in life due to a range of external or personal factors, and so may have a relatively limited repertoire of experience and thus relatively greater learning needs; second, the rate of change at this period of history (variously referred to as modernity or post-modernity) multiplies the challenges to everyone's store of experience, because so much of what has gone before no longer applies. As Jarvis (op. cit.) observes, for old people it is not only no longer the world they were born into, but scarcely the world that they retired into. This creates greater pertinence in the calculation for older people as to whether learning is possible and/or worth the effort (p. 167).

Motivations and purposes for later life learning

Given the potentially negative outcome outlined above, the purposes that do succeed to motivate older learners need to be considered. Jarvis (1989) concludes his argument with a typology of older learners, only one type of which opts for minimal learning (the 'harmony-seekers'). The other types he describes as 'the learners' and 'the doers'. The learners are the educational gerontologist's ideal types. As with people of every age they may not have the time or inclination to pursue every 'disjuncture', but they choose to engage with learning opportunities rather than settle for the restraints of the past. They have opportunity and motivation to select, to reflect, to be critical and to relate new information to previous experience.

The 'doers' are pursuing novelty and continuity in their activity rather than their conscious learning, which may be rejected for reasons of time, inclination, personal style, etc. Learning opportunities ('disjunctures') are dealt with by extending existing understanding (presumption) and by simply getting on with life (sports, travel, family, church, clubs, hobbies) for which their current repertoire is well equipped, and for which their knowledge can be deepened if not extended.

This is a contentious area of fine definition with which educators will continue to wrestle, and be accused of value judgement, no doubt. However, this attempt to conceptualise the link between experience and learning, which is particularly crucial in considering the older adult, may provide another angle for those explorations of non-participation in learning that gerontologists such as Weiland (1995) find so tedious (p. 40 this volume).

Assuming, however, that older adults can be engaged by educational opportunities (whether or not these result in learning) we can see that some programme purposes are going to be more interesting to different kinds of 'learners'. For example, some will be more motivated by learning to address particular new situations or roles, some to gain a general sense of intellectual exercise, some for the enjoyment of working in a group, some to pursue a particular academic or vocational goal.

Kolland (1993) proposes that one source of general motivation that would enable the 'proper stimulation of the learning processes' (p. 535) is the perception by older people of their learning ability. This perception has three aspects, which if taken on board can release desire for learning. First is the *consciousness that a person can act as a producer* of his/her own development by overcoming current barriers as well as past disadvantages in the learning career. Second, a *sense of competence to learn* is required that recognises itself as an 'ability to respond to the challenges of uncertain change in ill-structured surroundings' (p. 537) as opposed to comparing itself unfavourably with younger people. So saying, and thirdly, is the *acknowledgement* that the ability to develop oneself and demonstrate competence are *neither automatic nor mechanical*. They require effort and conscious pursuit.

This third, 'potential', aspect of older people's learning ability is perhaps the key to the process, if the conviction of ability (and thus motivation) to learn is to take hold. How else can a foothold be gained if, as has been suggested, older learners can be generally demotivated by their social circumstances and, thereby, their under-estimations of themselves? On the positive side for retirement, potential may be more easily identified by the individual who has been released from work-related roles or more instrumental learning.

Most commentators on older adults' learning mention this 'consciousness-raising' aspect as either a pre-requisite or an early effect of encounters with educational opportunities. Any difference here is entirely pragmatic, since it is well established that the experience of learning produces a desire for more. The success of the informal self-help model for later life learning testifies to the drawing in effect of an accessible and non-threatening introduction to education.

Peterson (1990) states that whatever form it takes, education for older adults is about 'helping people better understand and assist themselves' (p. 3). He also suggests that some so-called educational programmes might be more correctly described as recreation or diversion, despite their ability to play a helpful role in people's lives. (Perhaps these are the programmes for Jarvis' 'harmony seekers' or even his 'doers'?) Programmes that supply true educational purpose are those that facilitate people's attempts to understand and to know, thus taking effort, time and direction. Not wishing to claim the monopoly of educational programmes for such outcomes, Peterson notes that personal growth and development can also be achieved by pursuit of interests, and problems solved through conscious learning outside the confines of courses and relationships with an institution or 'teacher'.

Having said this, Peterson notes that, in addition to these private settings, a variety of institutional settings operate to offer multiple purposes and diverse outcomes for older learners. He suggests that these could be: preparation for new job, volunteer assignment or family role; psychological growth to explore innate (and untapped?) abilities; a mechanism to prevent physical, psychological or social decline; to evaluate lifelong experience and gain insight over its meaning (integration); to take the meaning discovered within knowledge and experience to a higher level of understanding (transcendence). Others have suggested (notably Erikson and Moody) that this last category of purpose is unique to later life.

The value of education to older adults is probably now well recognised, if not provided for. It is even supported in principle by policy makers who anticipate the benefits of both preventing decline and maximising potential in older people. Other positive later life effects could be continuing employability, better integration within society and changed demands on health and social services.

Self actualisation - the highest goal?

One focus in the debate about aims and purposes of education for seniors seems to be on the issue of self-actualisation and whether this is approachable directly through educational programming or whether preparing older people for activities and roles that might have self-actualising outcomes is the more effective way.

Chené and Fleury (1992) describe a college programme in Quebec which offered Diploma level studies with options in human science or arts to people aged 50, but whose 'prime objective was to facilitate self-actualisation at the time of retirement' (p. 499). The rationale for the curriculum was that socio-cultural education which focused on human relations would lead to a greater knowledge of self and enhanced social participation. An early goal of the programme, which took eight years to evolve to its current Diploma format, was 'the actualisation of the experiences of each participant and their immediate reinvestment in the community' (p. 499).

Other guiding principles underlying the programme identified by the authors were: a trust in older people's potential and the value of education to the process of transition; a conviction that personal development can be realised through acquiring knowledge and skills and that knowledge enables a 'reading of reality' with increased autonomy and ability to take action. Some of the outcomes of such a philosophy were the 'reappropriation of self'; and the ability to envisage and welcome change in life; an opportunity 'to enjoy a double-take on the meaning of life' (as opposed to preparation for entry into adult life); the expression of affective needs and recognition of the legitimacy of the older students' search for activities to further their well-being (p. 500-01). A conclusion is drawn that increasing knowledge and skills can offer people a means of reclaiming power over their lives and supporting them in their social roles.

In apparent contrast Manheimer and Snodgrass (1993) identify a more instrumental purpose for later life education. They draw a parallel between the women's movement out of which, as one result of greater consciousness concerning women's potential compared to their contemporary roles, there was a demand for education and training for new roles and greater participation in all spheres of public life.

> . . . today's older adults may be seeking pathways to new roles and new identities through renewal of the learning process and direction toward possible volunteer and entrepreneurial opportunities . . . linked to the older person's choice to stay or get involved in the community (p. 586).

Increasing pressure from retirees for life long learning helped establish the North Carolina Centre for Creative Retirement in 1987, Manheimer and Snodgrass claim, to provide 'life enrichment curricula' and 'institutional pathways to foster and channel the resourcefulness of older adults back into their communities'. Learning opportunities include peer learning and teaching (College for Seniors), and an intergenerational learning academy. The distinctive combination of college-based life long learning with leadership and community service programmes has led to a general appreciation of the new lifestyles of retirees and their social roles, as well as an increased self-consciousness among mid-lifers of the ageing process and the demands of retirement.

Such programmes have deliberately set out to meet the needs of largely middle-class seniors on the grounds that the new ranks of retirees seeking such learning are identified most usually by prior education. The percentage of college graduates amongst the older population is rising every year, along with the expectations of providers of life long education. The growing disparity in the distribution of educational opportunities within society, however, is a major cause for concern. Class, race and gender continue to limit prior access to learning in such a way that future cohorts of older people may not benefit in later life either.

From such observation, Manheimer and Snodgrass return to describing examples of provision such as 'community and personal awareness seminars preparing seniors to find meaningful volunteer positions', and drawing the conclusions that (i) colleges and universities can play a significant role in cultivating leadership, creativity and community service; (ii) there are growing numbers seeking such education and training; but (iii) older people still needed the incentive of a formal programme to encourage and facilitate their development of volunteer roles. The wider society into which seniors hoped to integrate new roles also needed a corresponding appreciation of what older people could contribute.

Manheimer and Snodgrass (1993) note that in order for this understanding to develop, society faces a range of new norms for later life. Taking two contrasting ones, a choice lay between the 'redemption', norm (whereby older people embraced age, accepted the inevitable, and demonstrated dignity and purpose for the end of life) and the 'social construction' norm (which enabled modification of a culturally imposed 'old age' and an invention of one's own version of retirement free of age-related expectations).

The authors conclude that the strong value of learning for older people was the opportunity it represented for reconsideration, renewal and reconnection regardless of whether the latter years required redeeming or liberating. Moreover, the practice of learning, in its different forms, needed to evolve with the demands of an ageing society, of which we have had little prior experience.

To conclude on self-actualisation which has been described as the highest goal of education for older adults, Bramwell (1992) discusses how education can be made relevant and meaningful for seniors. Where educational programmes are in a more *instructional or training mode* (conveying supposedly indispensable information, or teaching skills that lead to enhanced performance of some kind) then the programme's meaning and relevance must be demonstrated through the learning methodology, or selection of subject content. Experienced adults are more likely to question the point of various aspects of any educational experience than are younger learners.

If the educational programme is of another kind requiring, for instance, *inductive thought and reflection* rather than memorisation and performance, then older adults will be at an advantage. Notwithstanding, Jarvis' case for the differential quality of people's learning experiences and preferences, it can be generally supposed that older people will have greater experience of social values and norms and of interpreting the social environment. Such understandings form a valuable base for educational programmes that aims to initiate and follow-through lines of thought to form connections across subjects, to illuminate and exemplify from experience, producing 'recognition knowledge' as opposed to 'repetition knowledge'.

In practice, educational programmes will not usually exclusively reflect one type of learning or the other, as just described. Moreover, both can be achieved outside a formal learning group through reading, researching, or observing and conversing in everyday life. However, in seeking to elucidate the nature of effective and attractive learning opportunities for older people, Bramwell, as with others cited in this chapter, moves back and forth between the principles and the practice of education. In practice it is likely that there will be aims of instruction *and* induction. This is illustrated in the commentary on (pre) retirement education in Chapter 2, where the task to prepare for retirement has been variously interpreted as requiring 'indispensable information', skills, understanding and new ways of thinking.

How do such considerations link to the high goal of self-actualisation? McClusky (1974) suggested a helpful linkage, particularly influential in the USA, which provides a theoretical schema for the dilemmas of practitioners who aspire to such outcomes through their provision. With echoes of the hierarchies proposed by Maslow (1968) and by Erikson (1963), McClusky provides a listing of educational needs of older people, but with the difference that these need not be followed sequentially in order to be satisfied. They are simply descriptive of issues that can be addressed through learning in later life:

Coping, the capability to deal adequately with the physical, social and economic environment and the changes that occur in these spheres; *expressing*, not only communicating but also engaging in activities for the sake of it; *contributing*, playing a part in community or group life for the benefit of self as well as others; *influencing* others' views and treatment of oneself and one's peers, through formal and informal means; *transcending*, by rising above any perceived disadvantage of lesser power or life expectancy to recognise one's share and contribution on a broader human front.

> 'Psychologists, philosophers and educationists are at one in insisting that education for older persons should focus on self-fulfilment, self-actualisation, personal enrichment and self-transcendence, all of which go well beyond survival (Bramwell, 1992, p. 437).

Teaching and learning

Bramwell (op. cit.) relates his observations on the purposes and aims of education for seniors to conclusions about appropriate curriculum models. He contrasts traditional adult education approaches, typified by observable learning *outcomes*, with a range of alternative approaches but favouring one which stresses *input* and which relates more closely to the aims of initiating and inducing knowledge and understanding (already deemed to be of greatest importance to the older learner).

This latter 'input' model of the curriculum identifies worthwhile material, specifies ways that it is to be handled, anticipates various expected learning outcomes, but hopes for a further number of unexpected ones. Teachers will thus engage with mature students in a teaching / learning experience that appreciates more fully

> . . . the provisional and contextual nature of both public and private knowledge. The joint probing of teacher and student into motives, values and moral codes may reveal that these are culturally constructed . . . (and that) part of the hidden curriculum for seniors might be to engage in the critical analysis of received assumptions, common-sense knowledge and conventional behaviours (p. 445).

How then is the teacher to be best advised on how to engage in this learning partnership, whether seeking to offer instruction or induction? The potentially ambiguous role of the teacher of older students has been the subject of recent debate in British educational gerontology (see Glendenning and Percy, 1990). If the role involves engaging in the kind of critical analysis outlined above, which is widely supported in general terms by much of the literature discussed so far, then later life education will tend inevitably to raise consciousness about rights and roles as well as quality of life and self-actualisation.

For Battersby (1990) this leads logically to declaring a 'critical educational gerontology' which includes a concern for transforming the conditions that promote the disempowerment of older people, and to teaching practice that seeks to unsettle older people's assumptions that they cannot effect social change. Battersby (1993) develops the theme that anyone involved in older people's learning needs to recognise the ideological and ethical dimensions of their educational practice as well as the power relationships involved. (See Battersby and Glendenning in preparation for this series).

Withnall and Percy (1994) summarise and contrast this 'critical' position with that of the 'humanist' educator of older adults who facilitates the process of learning rather than necessarily seeking to persuade the student to social action, or even to unsettle their his/her assumption of lack of power. The humanist holds that educators have neither the right to take such a view of older people, nor the ability themselves to change power relations in society. Moreover the critical approach, which acknowledges the educational significance of older people's general disadvantage as a social -class, runs counter to the humanist's stress on learning as an individual quest and the imperative on the teacher to value and acknowledge each student's unique experience.

Glendenning (1990) attempts creatively to relate these two positions in order to prevent unhelpful polarisation. The critical approach does acknowledge and encourage the sharing of individual experience, he suggests, and does not assume disadvantage at the level of the individual. But the aim is to develop self-criticism, a questioning of existing knowledge, and a forging of new connections *from* the individual store of experience that the humanist teacher emphasises.

Older adults can then relate their extended knowledge to an understanding of power and its exercise. Whether or not a programme sets out to achieve this understanding may be a choice that the teacher or programme designer makes (operating on the 'outcomes' curriculum model that Bramwell describes) or may be one of the 'unexpected' results of his 'input' model, where the educational value lies in the process rather than the product. As Withnall and Percy (1994, p. 19) observe:

> educators need to be creative in finding ways to use the student's life experience to enhance the learning process. *The task is to integrate older people's experience into the conceptual structure of subject matter instead of sacrificing one to the other* (my emphasis).

The methods that are appropriate for this task of integration with older learners are often said to be different from those used with younger people. Apart from the greater store of experience, already discussed, Bolton (1990) suggests that two further significant factors differentiate teaching methods with middle aged and older adults. First, it must be appreciated that *individual differences* will predominate the teaching/learning process. Even with more formal or instructional programmes there will be diversity in the audience's educational needs and wants, expectations and purposes, styles and outcomes. This theme is explored by James (Chapter 5, this volume) but it is worth recalling that it is experience rather than chronological age per se that is the critical factor.

Second, *life course and cohort effects* complement individual differences (within generations) by demonstrating further dimensions of difference *between* generations due to historical events and prevailing contemporary conditions. Although there is little evaluative evidence about teaching strategies with older learners, Bolton (1990) nonetheless concludes that 'it would seem prudent to rely primarily on methods that emphasize individualisation of teaching and learning outcomes' (p. 139).

In practice, this will mean pursuing learner-focused methods rather than those which reflect a dependence on an external authority source, where the teacher directs the learning experience and the level of instruction is prescribed (and therefore pitched at the 'middle' ground of an heterogeneous group). In contrast, learner-centred methodologies allow the learning to be orchestrated rather than directed and instruction to be offered in a manner most useful to the learner, who in turn becomes more aware of the learning process through which (s)he is progressing.

The term andragogy was attributed in the 1970s to learner-centred approaches which were recognised as being best suited to the teaching of adults. Knowles' (1971) influential critique of traditional pedagogy and formulation of adragogical theory (and his subsequent development of the idea in 1973 and 1975) have been widely discussed and applied across the field of adult education. In 1983, Peterson made the application to the education of older adults, which has had a similarly important effect within educational gerontology (As further illustration, Coleman and Chiva 1991 and Walker 1992 made the application of adult learning methods to the practice of pre-retirement education).

Whilst the *theory* of older adults' independent learning skills and personal learning outcomes through the informed use of educational resources (including the teacher and the learning group) has enjoyed wide acceptance, its success *in practice* is less clear. Comparative evidence of the value of androgogical teaching and learning is extremely difficult to gather where overall provision, of whatever nature, is often local and/or temporary. A rare source of longitudinal data is now becoming available through the valuable work undertaken by the Older Students Research Group of the Open University (1984, 1987, 1994, 1995).

A short history of research into teaching and learning practice with older people is given in Withnall and Percy (1994) whose timely text explores the overall notion of what is meant by good practice in the education and training of older people. Since they illustrate their arguments with examples of practice, the issue of provision will not be pursued here. Suffice it to say that such studies as have been carried out have illustrated, if not fully taken into account, the 'multitude of confounding factors involved in evaluation of outcomes' for older learners (Bolton, p. 139). The design of teaching strategies for experienced adult learners is far mor complex than many would expect, he suggests.

The Carnegie Inquiry into the Third Age reported (inter alia) on education, training and information available to third agers (defined as 50-75 years). The variety and ad hoc nature of provision was accompanied by a dearth of evaluative data which made comparison and, thus, trends difficult to identify. Schuller and Bostyn (1992) recommend that basic indicators of effectiveness be planned and operationalised by providers of older adults' learning, such as enrolment and completion records, student outcomes, forms of progression, qualifications or competencies gained etc, (and equivalent measures would need to be designed for informal learning). They also suggest a range of research methods that would help generate reliable data on older people's learning, so that dissemination and comparison of findings can help to build up the field of study, and generate new theory and practice. Despite his pessimism about the complexity of designing effective learning opportunities, Bolton concludes that'methodology design must become more individualised, more creative than a technical process and probably most important, de-schooled' (p. 143). There is creative potential in curriculum design, he feels, which is vital for the experience of later life, about which gerontology is discovering more at an increasing rate. The developmental demands of retirement and ageing are largely dependent for their fulfilment on the achievement of new learning, in whatever way this can be done.

A reformed adult education, appropriate to meeting such demands by older learners, would challenge the tendency towards habitual information processing; enhance the learner's sense of control and power through knowledge; promote a belief in the value of education in making life better and in the possibility of educational achievement, together producing a high sense of 'educational efficacy'; enhance learners' intentions to produce self-initiation and goal-setting; remove from methodology any schooling-related or traditional notions that prevent the incorporation of what is now understood about older learners' wants and needs; acknowledge the social learning tasks that older people face in developing new roles, and in dealing with change and transition.

Rights and opportunities

In 1986, Liddington shared her thoughts about developing learner-centred adult education for older people in the Bradford area of Yorkshire.

> I began to work out in my own mind why older adults should be more involved in adult education. Was it because their educational needs were so much greater than those of younger people? Or because they had established rights to education, by dint of paying their rates and taxes all their working lives? Or because if they weren't offered education they would be less able to live independent lives, and so be increasingly dependent on the state and community? (p. 138).

Withnall and Percy (1994) note that the philosophies that inspired educational gerontology were those that made a case for extending adult and continuing education and training to older people, often on the grounds of previous lack of opportunity, or on grounds of entitlement as citizens participating in society. The trap of then portraying older learners as disadvantaged, in special need, suffering deficits and disempowerment of their rights, was a real danger.

Some early provision worked within such thinking in order to secure special funding, but the short-lived nature of support that was so subject to local and national policy change was eventually seen as disadvantageous. Critiques were emerging (see, for example, Cooper and Bornat's 1988 infamously titled article

Combatting the Woolly Bunny) of providing for older learners on the basis of their disadvantage, although elements of this approach are still to be found wherever certain policy outcomes are seen as desirable (e.g. less long-term unemployment, less psychosomatic illness, or reduced inter-generational conflict etc.).

Assuming, then, that the trap of the disadvantage label can be avoided, the moral and philosophical arguments can be examined for their current force.

The case for entitlement to educational opportunities often rests on a comparison of rights accrued through payment of taxes and contribution to national productivity, with the relative lack of service received due to historical cohort effects (world war, economic depression, the late expansion of higher education, etc). Generational inequalities, penalising particular cohorts, have also been compounded for many of today's seniors by the unequal distribution of educational opportunities in societies stratified by class and gender as well as age. The argument for equity of treatment is therefore part of the overall case for entitlement. Liddington (1986) comments that a typical student involved with her educational outreach programme in Bradford was a single elderly woman, living alone, on state pension only, having left school at 14 or younger, and having had no chance to take part in an identifiable learning programme since that time.

When the climate of education and training is so instrumental (and thus future-oriented) in intent, if not in actual content, it may be difficult to press an argument for entitlement based on past contributions. The question of future benefit will remain unsatisfied, unless the case for learning as an end in itself can become more widely accepted. Education for older people could then be legitimately claimed as a prize to which all ages and generations can aspire. Claiming on the grounds of past citizenship inequities needs to be supplemented by grounds of current citizenship entitlement *whether or not one's participation is deemed to be productive* by society.

A further angle on equitable access to learning is taken by those who argue that, irrespective of the past, older adults require equal opportunities here and now (to formal education, to training for jobs, to educational guidance, etc). The case is that, as for gender and race, discrimination and loss of opportunity on grounds of an ascribed class characteristic is not only ethically unacceptable, but also harmful to society by denying life chances to competent contributors to its well-being. The anti-ageism stance is essentially a demand for a level playing field not one for special or remedial treatment. In this regard, age as an equal opportunity issue links to a broader line of thought about human rights, which seeks to recognise intrinsic human value and legitimate claims on society, regardless of personal or group circumstances. You cannot deserve or earn human rights, and the case for restoring them to a deprived group is not necessarily stronger than for maintaining them for any other group.

A different way of viewing and crediting the past in relation to the present and future is expressed by those concerned with intergenerational solidarity. An underlying assumption is that an intergenerational contract exists whereby support is both given and received reciprocally over a lifetime so that each succeeding generation can expect a return on their contributive phases. Great concern currently exists around the potential for conflict where older or younger generations perceive inequity in either the input or output calculations. The future of social security through pension systems is the particular focus of intergenerational concern in most developed nations, but the general framework for the just distribution of social assets applies more widely to other forms of services and support, such as access to education. Laslett and Fishkin (1992) bring concepts of social philosophy and the law to bear on the question of justice between age groups and generations in an unprecedented era where ageing societies are beginning to question whether the intergenerational contract can meet the new demands put upon it.

Lastly, a more pragmatic case for older adults' learning is emerging from the needs of society to become a 'learning culture', rather than from the needs of its members as a primary consideration. Withnall and Percy (1994) describe how economic imperatives have changed the framework of education and training for adults generally, because of the need for a more highly trained and flexible workforce. Lifelong learning no longer needs defending as a concept. The nature of the workforce is being redefined by demographic factors in manpower supply, and by the disappearance of careers which used to offer continuous or at least progressive experiences of employment.

All members of society, of a wide range of ages, will need to be equipped with broad-based skills to enable employment and/or further education to take place. Future cohorts of third agers ('retiree' is a difficult concept in this context) will thus be better placed to demand further learning. Moreover, such a scenario implies the subsuming of older adults' learning as a distinctive activity into a life-long learning culture. As Withnall and Percy note, the current vocational version on offer of life-long learning would need to broaden considerably before it could serve the needs of older learners.

5 Adapting and surviving: Some implications for pre-retirement education

David James

In his pioneering book, *Human Learning* Edward Thorndike (1931) wrote 'In learning resides humanity's power to change, possibly the most impressive of human gifts.'

The world around us, and indeed our own lives are constantly changing at, it is often claimed, an ever-increasing rate. Our ability to survive, cope with and benefit from these changes depends to a very large extent on our competence to develop our understanding of new situations, to acquire additional relevant skills and knowledge, perhaps to change our attitudes or priorities or our habitual patterns of behaviour. In other words we must learn and go on learning throughout our lives.

All this is extremely important for what we call pre-retirement education (PRE). PRE in Britain emerged in the 1950s and 1960s as a result of empirical research findings by clinical psychologists working for the Medical Research Council. They concluded that industrial workers suffered from stress as the time for the cessation of full-time paid work approached. In those days 'retirement' was at 60 or 65. Now it is the norm for few men to be in full-time paid work after 60 and in the economic recession of the 1970s and 1980s, redundancy and what is euphemistically still called 'early retirement' became an all to familiar experience. At the end of the 1950s, Heron, who was later to become an internationally respected clinical psychologist, suggested a series of topics which should be discussed with employees prior to retirement, to prepare them for the sudden change in lifestyle. These topics included adequate income, health, suitable accommodation, leisure activities and interests and congenial relationships.

With the development of the pre-retirement movement in the mid-1960s, these topics became the ones most favoured by those who organised pre-retirement 'courses'. In addition the organisers and presenters were invariably people without

61

educational experience and by the mid-1970s there was a 'rebellion' by adult educators and psychologists about the content of pre-retirement education (PRE) and the methodology employed. PRE in practice had come to be seen by employers and organisers as a means of giving information rather than engaging retirees in facing the process of change. The call for the rethinking of PRE led to two major university-based research projects which recommended many changes if the process of PRE was to be a helpful and creative experience. The British Pre-Retirement Association was recognised with government funding by the then Department of Education and Science from 1983 onwards. This has enabled it to create a coherent approach to retirement issues and to develop professional standards both in content and methodology.

Although our capacity to learn is highly developed, it may not always be adequate to meet the demands placed upon it. This is particularly the case when extensive or traumatic changes are suddenly imposed upon us and for which we have not prepared ourselves. Retirement, like redundancy or bereavement can still be experienced these days as a major upheaval occurring in mid to later life. If the psychological and social patterns of many years are suddenly rendered irrelevant or inappropriate the individual is likely to feel lost or disoriented and consequently to be extremely vulnerable. That 'dynamic equilibrium' which is the hallmark of good health and adjustment may be substantially upset. Pre-retirement preparation assumes that we are likely to be able at least to avoid the worst excesses of such changes and indeed, by helping individuals to help themselves, to grow through the experience and benefit from it.

We will therefore consider here some basic aspects of how we learn and how we can help ourselves and each other to learn to cope with, enjoy and prosper in retirement.

Learning and change

Learning is so ubiquitous that we tend to take if for granted and, particularly in adult life, do not realise how much we rely on it. Its importance in childhood is more obvious, where we are aware of how rapidly infants develop through experience and practice, learning to crawl, stand, walk and talk. At school, youngsters learn society's language, culture, system of values, morality and customs. They are being prepared for adult life (traditionally a life of work) which will be spent in a world in which language, art, customs, law, science, religion and all the achievements of civilisation are the results of human experience and learning.

Learning in mid and later life draws from and builds on earlier learning

(Cunningham and Brookbank, 1988). This process is likely to be easier and more effective where there is some continuity, where the demands remain similar to those for which we have been prepared and which are familiar to us. But what if major discontinuity occurs? Can we suddenly put aside previous learning which is no longer relevant? Can we quickly and effectively acquire new and different ways of interpreting, thinking, prioritising, responding? Can we replace previously held attitudes and values that are no longer relevant? Do we need to adapt and, if so, do we need help in so doing? These are questions which those approaching retirement and those concerned with providing for preparation for retirement need to consider.

The need for and competence of adults to cope with major discontinuities in their lives is a subject of great concern and interest in many social spheres ranging from international problems of migration between and integration into different cultures, to the personal promotion prospects for individuals in employment. Take, for example, criteria for advancement within the nursing profession. The newly qualified practitioner is primarily concerned with hands-on, patient care. If he/she is successful at this level, then promotion to first line management (ward sister / charge nurse) may follow. Here the role changes to giving direct supervision to others doing the job which the individual has already mastered. Further promotion may mean that the sphere of influence of the individual becomes so wide that he/she can only scan the whole and focus in on important or difficult issues as they arise. Success at this level, however, still depends to a great extent for competence and credibility on having previously successfully fulfilled the roles of the staff now being managed (Elliot, 1993).

If major changes are to be introduced into the system in terms of philosophy, policy and practices (e.g. from patient-centred to cost-centred management) can those who have grown up and become steeped in the old tradition provide leadership into the new regime? Alternatively, should people from outside the health service who are used to the new system operating elsewhere where financial considerations dominate thinking, be brought in as new leaders? In many public services, policy formers and decision makers, be they senior executives, governors or directors are increasingly being drawn from commerce and private industry, a situation experienced by many nationalised industries in the past.

While the example given above is concerned primarily with the perceived difficulty of changing professional attitudes after long experience of a particular employment culture, clearly the same kind of argument can be used in relation to personal dimensions of life. If an individual has spent many years in a job which has had a major influence on almost every aspect of his/her life from the reason for getting up in the morning, and the structure of the day, week and year to issues of status and security, companionship and interest, then can all this be put to one side and a new set of goals, priorities and values be accepted?

Is such a fundamental re-orientation necessary? Just as many managers would argue that there is no need to truncate their professional development because of far-reaching changes in the job for which they are employed, so many people approaching retirement feel quite relaxed and positive about the changes ahead. This is particularly the case for those whose life has several different components to it. Allatt (see Walker, 1992 and also p. 34 this volume) has proposed the concept of 'life strands' as an interesting model for viewing the development of the individual. She suggests that we each have several strands relating to our employment, domestic life, leisure, health and so on, and that as time goes by, these expand and/or contract according to circumstances. If we have several well-established and developed strands we can cope with the loss of one through the expansion of the others, more easily than if one strand (here employment) completely dominates and so when we lose it (by retirement) our lives become empty, lacking in goals or purposes. This picture is exacerbated by the fact that for such single-minded people, work is likely to have been their main source of identity for most of their lives. To lose that identity, and consequently their sense of personal value and of having a worthwhile contribution to make to society when they retire, is very hard to bear.

The nature of learning

What do we mean by 'learning'? Although the process is often defined in terms of 'changes in behaviour resulting from experience', it is important to realise that these behavioural changes are just a convenient practical way of identifying that some kinds of learning (those reflected in behaviour) have occurred. When we receive experiences from the world around us, we take selectively from them and integrate this selected material into our existing knowledge and ideas in a complex, cumulative manner. Consequently, the internal world which each of us constructs and against which we interpret external events contains a great deal of material which is largely independent of the current external environment and which reflects our experiences of earlier times (Woods and Brittan, 1985). If these times were very different from the present our current interpretations may be inappropriate or unhelpful. We may attempt to ignore or dismiss the new experiences, or force them into a perceptual mould which fits our existing ideas but which, in effect, distorts reality. In either case the result is likely to be unhelpful in enabling the individual to adjust to and cope with the new situation being encountered. On the other hand, where people have experience which relates to or can be adapted to the new situation, it is likely that they will approach it more positively, interpret it more accurately and be able to respond to it more effectively (See also the discussion of learning and later life in Chapter 4, this volume).

This is, of course, the premise on which much pre-retirement preparation is based but before considering its practical implications it is worth examining some of the psychological processes involved in a little more detail. Our brains are limited in many ways in relation to the demands we make upon them. We cannot remember all that we want to remember or solve all the problems that we want to solve. Relevant to the current discussion, we cannot assimilate all the information bombarding our sense organs at any one time. We must select from it and our brains are programmed to focus our senses on those parts of the environment which are likely to be important to us.

We all, for example, pay attention to stimuli which have potential survival relevance to us. We have evolved, in line with many other species, the tendency to pay attention to parts of the environment which are unusual, where things are happening or which make an intense impact. We can generally afford to ignore situations which are familiar, where the status quo is being maintained and which make little impact. So when we want to attract attention to ourselves in an emergency we might shout and wave our arms, or to a fire engine. We construct it to have dynamic, intrusive qualities such as being big, red and noisy with flashing lights and two-tone sirens. If we want to avoid attracting attention or to camouflage something we do the reverse. Most people will attend to the same features of a situation in-so-far-as these particular characteristics are concerned.

On the other hand, we also pay attention to stimuli which have the potential to satisfy our needs or which relate to our personal interests. These will vary from person to person. Insecure individuals will see threats all around them, the sexually deprived can be obsessionally interested in the opposite gender, a person with an enthusiasm for a particular hobby, say natural history, will notice many details of the countryside that most of us miss. This example brings in a third category of items that will attract our attention, namely stimuli we have learned to select because we have found that they have relevance to our lives, our work or our interests. The information to which we attend both reflects our personal inner world and tends to reinforce and strengthen it.

This inner world of personal interpretation is then used to anticipate and predict what will happen next, to estimate which new information is likely to be significant for us, and to determine how we should respond. These selective processes enable us to deal with a volume of information far exceeding our capacity to receive or process it. It means, however, that we have partial and unique interpretations of the world around us (Cunningham and Brookbank, op. cit). Yet we tend to operate on the basis that we share complete interpretations which are common to us all. What we see is largely determined by what we want to see (reflecting our personal needs) and what we expect to see (reflecting our personal experiences) Pre-retirement educators have to consider what this means for people contemplating or coping with retirement whose experience to date has come from a life of employment and whose outlook, attitudes and desires are (assumed to be) still work-related.

In summary of this section, then, we can each assimilate large quantities of experience into our mental life that can sustain itself with a considerable degree of autonomy, giving us independence from our environments to explore, to choose and to make important decisions about our lives. This freedom of thought and action is characteristic of mankind and is part of what makes us 'human'. Take away that autonomy and the individual feels less than human, a major problem for many older people if they become decreasingly self-sufficient.

Learning and pre-retirement education

Our discussion of learning as a process demonstrates its fundamental and wide-ranging effect on other mental processes. What we attend to (which information we select), how we perceive (how we interpret situations), what motivates (stimulates) us to thought or action, what we know, think, remember, and to a very considerable extent, the kinds of people (personalities) we are, all depend heavily on our past experience.

It is however not only what we have learned but also how we have learned to learn which is important. The formal education mode current when people who are today reaching retirement age were still at school tended to be very traditional in that it was teacher-centred, solution-centred and essentially passive. The value of such an approach is clear for the speedy acquisition of skills or information which once mastered can be used with increasing facility the more often they are practised. Its limitation, however, is that it is not very helpful in many real life situations where the 'learner' has no 'teacher' to emulate, where he/she is presented with a problem rather than a solution and where progress will be made only through the individual's own actions. Learner-centred, problem-solving, active learning is the norm for most of us throughout our adult lives. For many who found the school approach difficult and as a result suffered at their teachers' hands, the idea of 'being taught' is greeted with negative feelings. For them particularly learning based on real life, demonstrably valuable and successful ways of coping with their own lives by solving their own problems will not only be more acceptable but more effective.

Let us consider briefly how people learn about 'new' topics of interest to them. 'New' is often a relative term. If a topic is completely new e.g. a foreign language never encountered before, or scientific or mathematical subject being studied for the first time, it is possible that the learner would have little relevant past experience and so would be entirely dependent on someone else be it a teacher, author, programme producer or whoever. In subjects normally encountered in a pre-retirement programme or publications, however, it is unlikely that entirely new material will constitute much of the content. Course participants or readers will, more likely, need to reflect on their own experience, share it with others to see alternative or additional perspectives, and interpret and identify issues which they want to pursue (and opportunities for pursuing them) in order to adapt their current thinking to their new and changing circumstances.

Thinking about this from the point of view of the provider of learning opportunities we can see the 'teaching strategy' as helping new learners who are initially to some degree dependent on others to achieve greater independence in terms of handling their own experience, sorting out priorities and becoming re-oriented if necessary, so that they feel that they can stand on their own feet and take responsibility for themselves in the new context. Only when a person has achieved some degree of autonomy or independence of thought is he/she likely to be able to make a full contribution from a position of strength to a group, course, or indeed community. Out of such an interdependent, co-operating, sharing group, some individuals may emerge with 'leadership' qualities, but it is to be hoped that all will be capable of further self-directed growth.

The above encapsulates the sort of development which will usually underlie curriculum or editorial planning and decision-making about pre-retirement education material. Obviously, things can go wrong. For example, an individual may feel so insecure in relation to impending retirement that he/she demonstrates helplessness, withdrawn or aggressively unconstructive behaviour. He/she may feel isolated, alone and rejected and far from being open to new ideas and opportunities in the new life opening up, demonstrate anger, frustration and other negative feelings. Many other examples of intra- and inter-personal problems can be cited. The purpose here is to consider how effective learning can be achieved in preparation for retirement, while noting that for many reasons difficulties may arise which need to be identified and dealt with in the context of the opportunities provided.

Effective learning involves integrating new, relevant information into the already existing, well-developed inner self in a meaningful, acceptable manner which does not create unnecessary or excessive dissonance. As each individual is unique in his/her experiences, needs, interests, concerns, learning strategies must be designed to allow different individuals to take quite different things from the opportunities provided. While this may appear to be stating the obvious, it is often apparently not considered when for example highly structured, speaker-centred programmes are provided on pre-retirement courses.

Let us take, as an illustration, a lecture on 'health in retirement'. Different individuals will have different strengths and limitations, understanding and fears in relation to the topics covered. What they attend to (and what they miss) will differ accordingly. How they organise or adapt this new material into their own inner selves may therefore be quite inappropriate in some cases, but without feedback through discussion and clarification, this will not be realised by anyone (especially the course member). The inner self is the centre in which our personal thinking, reasoning, imagining takes place. A person getting hold of the wrong end of the stick can be greatly worried by a general statement made by a professional in a context in which sharing of concerns is both difficult and inappropriate. Instead the individual may rehearse, and extend his/her misinterpretation to considerable personal detriment. These same problems clearly may be experienced in any sphere where new information is presented in a passive, solution-centred format.

Adult educators would contend that strategies increase the effectiveness of learning when they offer a planned sequence of activities appropriate to the subject and based on an understanding of the needs and abilities of the learner. What is important is activity, both to ensure relevant integration of new ideas with existing learning and to give feedback to the individual and others of the effectiveness of this integration. This effectiveness does not depend on the individual deliberately following a learning strategy or being aware of following a lesson plan, or even having a deliberate intention to learn. The requirement is to engage on some activity that involves him/her in processing items in a way which is meaningful to the inner self and which reinforces, extends or otherwise modifies it (Kogan, 1990).

Conclusion

In much current thinking about adult education there is a tendency to assume that improvements in learning can be achieved by simply creating stimulating learning environments. As we have considered in this chapter, effective learners are highly active individuals exploring and experimenting with their surroundings. They construct their knowledge, understanding, inner selves through interaction with the external world. Experience is the outcome of this interaction. Consequently providing an individual with a course or publication or resource centre full of information will not necessarily mean that he/she learns very much. Experiences which most strongly influence what we learn are determined by how we act in the context of the experiences.

Take, for example, learning a foreign language. This is much more effective where it increases our chances of coping with the environment, where we get feedback and where we grow in confidence. So we are likely to learn much more quickly and easily when we are in the country where the language is spoken and we have to use it to survive. This is a clear familiar example of active integration of new material with clear knowledge of results. It applies equally to pre-retirement education.

We depend on the external world but are not slaves to it. The active nature of learning means that there is choice for us in how and what we learn, and that each of us will construct a world of experience unique to ourselves. Pre-retirement preparation is fundamentally concerned with helping individuals to reflect on their own inner worlds, to consider their adequacy for meeting present and future needs and to facilitate, where appropriate, personal action to build on strengths and make good deficiencies as identified by the individuals themselves.

6 Managing change in mid and later life

Anthony Chiva

This chapter adopts a psychological standpoint in order to review the way an individual's potential at birth, together with the developmental and maintenance processes (which will be discussed with reference to the concept of dynamic holism) function to meet environmental challenges, and how they operate throughout life and into retirement.

An assumption is made that the majority of human beings are born with the potential ability to function effectively in all circumstances, that is, with an inner awareness of themselves and their surroundings, and an innate ability to adapt and function holistically. All elements of the new human being function to create an individual capable of positive action, self-actualisation and unconditional regard or love (Jackins, 1981).

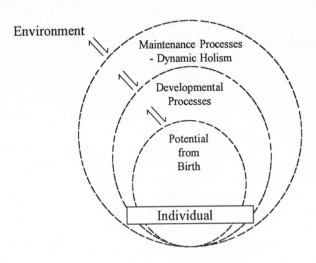

Figure 6.1   **The individual and the environment**

Unfortunately this potential is often not fully achieved. The innate adaptability, which responds creatively to produce a perfectly competent individual, also responds to perceived negative environmental circumstances in which the human infant finds itself. In these negative situations the child adapts to 'hurts', negative criticism, or inappropriate parenting such that his/her competence becomes reduced, though never lost. By the time people become adults their conscious self-perception is often limited. People reaching the third age with feelings of low self-esteem, for example, are perhaps embracing negative messages or 'scripts' about their lives (Berne, 1964).

The individual constantly creates and recreates itself in the interplay with the environment. If it is the case that the individual is a reflection of their experiences within this persona (interaction of self with others) then personality can be seen as being largely learned. This applies to most of the elements (Figure 6.2), excluding the genetic contribution and the limits thereby placed through physiology.

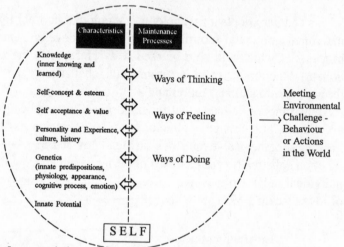

Figure 6.2 Self and characteristics

In terms of developmental processes as the infant grows, primary socialisation (within the home) and secondary socialization (within school) takes place. Through these processes the child's psychological attributes become redefined and re-programmed, and ways of thinking are learned. It has been proposed that there is a need to complete key developmental or life tasks at certain stages. Erikson (1963) has suggested eight stages (Table 6.1). Successful completion of these stages, he believed, would enable better adjustment to change. So that if Stage One is not successfully completed the individual may not feel able to form new relationships or detach from the old ones irrespective of their quality. People can move into later stages of life with uncompleted life tasks, but this will hinder adjustment, reduce confidence and is more likely to lead to resistance to letting-go. Erikson considered that life tasks can be completed later than the expected age, although this requires conscious effort and some personal commitment.

Table 6.1
Stages of development, after Erikson

Stage One
Basic Trust v. Mistrust:Infancy (0-1 year)
In this stage a child has the opportunity to develop trust. If this does not happen the child will grow up distrusting the world and maybe itself.

Stage Two
Autonomy v. Shame & Doubt:Early Childhood (1 - 3 years)
In these years a child seeks to explore the world, from the security established in the first year. If at this stage if it is humiliated or unsupported, the autonomy is less likely to develop.

Stage Three
Initiative v. Guilt:Childhood (3 - 6 years)
In this stage a child will be adventurous and take risks, unless they are discouraged and treated as 'bad' for doing such things.

Stage Four
Industry v. Inferiority:Middle Childhood (6 - 12 years)
During this stage confidence builds, and effort is put into tasks and work. Confidence is demonstrated.

Stage Five
Identity v. Role Confusion:Adolescence (13 - 22 years)
In this period young people are concerned about what others think of them. They undergo major physiological changes and are required to develop their own identity as distinct from that of family or friends.

Stage Six
Intimacy v. Isolation:Young Adulthood (22 - 30 years)
If the ego identity has formed then individuals can safely develop intimacy. They would not feel threatened by someone else's closeness or power. If this is less successful the ability to commit oneself to another person regardless of the results is unlikely.

Stage Seven
Generativity v. Stagnation:Middle Adulthood (30 - 50 years)
In this stage the individual is ready to help others to learn and understand.

Stage Eight
Integrity v. Despair:Late Adulthood (50 + years)
Acceptance of life that has been lived, and making sense of experience.

According to Erikson's thinking there is an opportunity for greater competence through successful completion of life tasks. Given that people sometimes need to take 'later' opportunities for successful life task completion, the third age can provide such an opportunity for resolution, and the maintenance processes provide the means.

Riker and Myers (1990) suggest that there are additional life tasks after 50+ years. These life tasks are considered to relate to the different arenas or 'strands' in an individual's life, such as social, financial, work, health etc., which can be conceived as separate but lifelong 'careers' which interact over time. Within these and other such areas that could be defined, the life task of 50+ is primarily the need for 'ego transcendence'. This task has two main parts: firstly the need to look beyond oneself and identify the things that are to be left behind for others (for children, the community, and society); and second to identify and link with a power outside oneself. Without the accomplishment of this transcendence the individual may not consider their life a success, and may fear their own death. For some this may mean not living life to the full. In the late adulthood stage, of course, it must be recognised that many people do deem themselves successes in life, and are deemed so by others, even though they still have 'unfinished business'.

Psychological development is considered by other humanistic psychologists (e.g. Berne 1964) somewhat differently. According to his transactional analysis (TA) approach, as children interact with their environment they acquire fundamental attitudes to themselves and others. Through a series of unsuccessful 'transactions' with others, an individual may adopt a 'negative life script', such as feeling unloved. They would then lead their future lives so that this becomes their reality. In a similar way, an individual may decide they are 'not OK' (Harris, 1969), they are a bad or undeserving person. This severely affects the way the individual conducts life and social relations and, again, expectation may be fulfilled. Unless the individual consciously breaks the cycle of negative self-view, then continuing negative expectation and negative behaviour will lead to a negatively scripted outcome.

Transactional analysis suggests a means by which individuals can overcome negatively-conditioned concepts and attitudes by considering the messages they give and receive and the way these show themselves in every-day life. TA encourages the individual to review their perceived self and to reconsider their fundamental attitudes and beliefs, which were adopted out of awareness when a child. Attitudes and beliefs originally formed for defence may now be no longer protective but possibly self-damaging. Berne, like Erikson, believes that people can acquire new attitudes and behaviours and become 'winners' in their interactions with the world, thus making continuing development in later life a possibility.

The fundamental beliefs that an individual holds about him/herself can be reinforced or challenged by other people and situations in which they find themselves, especially where the mature adult is aware of his/her current life-task as a motivation for, or as a result of, change. Often mid-life is a time of review, of comparing expectations against actual achievements when differences become dramatic. This process has been exacerbated by recent changes in employment practice increasing the likelihood of job change / loss in later adulthood. In these changing economic circumstances it becomes even more relevant for individuals to manage change positively.

At this time the interplay between the elements of the self making up the maintenance processes come into play, especially through a process that can be termed 'dynamic holism'.

Dynamic holism describes the process by which the individual maintains a dynamic balance between the different aspects of themselves. Figure 6.3 shows the main components of the self. Balancing the self therefore involves integrating ways of thinking, feeling, behaving/doing and socialising, also taking physical dimensions of the self into account.

The concept of dynamic holism enables the level of an individual's functioning, or health or wellness to be described in a multifaceted manner. The whole person is highly complex and it may be that an individual would describe themselves as functioning at a high social level and a lower physical level. In this case the dynamic balance is shifted away from the physical self.

Figure 6.3   Dynamically balanced aspects of self

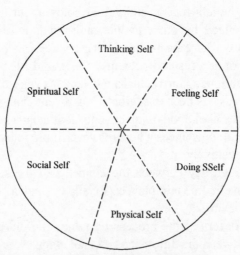

Figure 6.4 Shifting balance I: high social, low physical

Alternatively, an individual may have high order functioning in thinking, and lower functioning in the social self. Shifting the dynamic balance away from the social self.

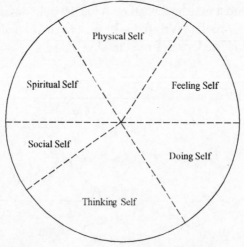

Figure 6.5 Shifting balance II: high thinking, low social

The balance may temporarily settle as indicated in Figures 6.4 and 6.5, however with change there can be a dynamic shift to a new balance. The individual is multidimensional and health could be seen to be at a high level in some areas and lower in others. This concept therefore allows for both the high level wellness model (Dunn, 1973) or the salutogenic (as opposed to pathological) model of health (Antonovsky, 1979).

The implications of the dynamic holism model are that:

- The individual seeks to create a balance at which adequate functioning can take place.
- The level/place of balance will vary with different aspects of the self.
- The individual strives to establish balance which changes and shifts over time, with changing emphasis.
- The level of wellness will vary with different aspects of the person.
- Re-establishing balance is always possible.
- It is possible to increase the level of functioning and wellness at any time.
- The different aspects of self interrelate and are interdependent.

Dynamic holism therefore involves balance being maintained between all aspects of the person. In this chapter the main focus will be on psychological aspects.

An individual faced with a life change in their mid or later life will bring 'themselves' (at their current state of development) to the situation. The following abilities, or 'tools' can be thought of/conceived as making up a personal skills bank. These may need to be sharpened in order to manage change at a higher level of competence, thus shifting the balance in a positive direction.

These abilities or 'tools' (which constitute the maintenance processes) include:

cognitive processing : ways of thinking
emotional processing : ways of feeling
behavioural processing : ways of doing

These 'tools' include the following skills:
assessment;
handling changes;
self-acknowledgment and self-reward;
caring for oneself;
stress management;
communication;
negotiation;
assertiveness;
gaining support;
application of personal philosophy.

The ease or comfort an individual has with themselves (ie their acceptance of themselves as they are), almost irrespective of life change, marks an important starting point in managing challenging situations. The development of self acceptance is vital and relates to the individual gaining a better understanding of themselves, and in achieving the transcendence that Erikson and others have defined as important in later life.

The implications for development in later life of the three processes (thinking, feeling and doing) and their associated skills (see above) will now be considered in greater detail.

Cognitive processing: ways of thinking

The cognitive process is a relatively complex interaction involving some key cognitions such as thinking, intuiting, willing and knowing.

The thinking process is dependent on the way the individual has learned to see the world and select information from it. In this sense, cognitive processes are constructed and mediated by the environment and its challenges, as well as the individual's inherited capacities. Before any thought takes place, either consciously (in awareness) or subconsciously (out of awareness) the perceptual system (senses and brain) has selected the information received.

In terms of patterns of thinking('learned thinking') problems may have arisen when thinking has been judged 'irrational' (see under emotional processing). Thoughts *about* perceptions take place along pathways / routes that have been established. These enable comparisons with previous experience or currently held attitudes and beliefs. For example, in terms of the changing seasons, this may involve recognition and matching from experience of trees in the summer, winter, spring and autumn. In terms of attitudes and values it may involve a like or dislike of a particular season for being cold and depressing or sharp and crisp. The *thought* of winter is linked to existing attitudes, beliefs and values.

In meeting changes in life, the learned thinking process may link to a wider range of previous experiences, attitudes, beliefs and values, and relate to longer-standing mental constructs and individual world views, (see Kelly, 1963). The strength of these beliefs and values may be greater concerning personal life change than, for instance, about seasons. The nature of the thinking process will determine the way life change is viewed.

The process of 'cognitive evaluation' has been put forward by Cox (1978). He proposes that this is a process whereby the perceived ability of the individual is weighed against the perceived demand required by different aspects of change. If, in the cognitive evaluation, the perceived demand is greater than the perceived ability to manage it, then the change will be seen as stressful with associated negative attributes. If, on the other hand, the perceived demand of the change is seen to be equal to perceived ability, then the change will be seen as a positive challenge and even welcomed as an opportunity for growth and revitalisation.

It is important to note that, in this process of cognitive evaluation, it is not the real demand or real ability that is evaluated. The perception of the individual therefore determines the resultant psychological and physiological effects of the change. This means that an individual has the opportunity to reframe, or redefine, the way they perceive the demands within the change as well as the way they perceive their own abilities to meet these demands.

Practically this can be achieved in a number of ways, and involves assessing the situation more objectively. An example of this would be the application of the Managing Change Model as described by Coleman and Chiva (1991). Another objective cognitive approach is given in Hayes and Hopson (1976) who also suggest that it is helpful to view change more as gains than losses. They add that the way a change is viewed, based on personal orientation and experience, determines the ease of managing the change. They suggest that the following will help support change management: Understanding the change; seeing the change more as a gain than a loss; and managing the stress.

Other mental processes require mention here. Those such as intuition and 'inner knowing' contribute significantly to the way an individual can exert a dynamic balance within themselves and their environment. In terms of a holistic view of a person, the contribution of these processes may be critical. In a person who is developing acceptance and self-awareness, the acknowledgement and recognition of ways of knowing (such as intuition and spiritual or psychic processes) can be essential. These aspects of self-development require an openness and desire to perceive oneself within a broad context.

For further discussion of these issues see: Seddon, 1993; Brusselmans, et al., 1980; Jarvis and Walters, 1993, and *Making the Most of Your Retirement: a workbook*, Chiva (1995).

Since changes do involve gains and losses, the effects of these on the ability to process the emotional aspects of psychological functioning need to be explored. Enhancement of skills in this area is of great value at any age. (see Cox 1978 on emotional responses to cognitive appraisal).

Emotional processing

A starting point in this process is the acceptance that all feelings are valid. Key steps in emotional processing are:

- Recognising and acknowledging feelings in oneself
- Understanding the feelings
- Looking after oneself during, or as soon as possible, with respect to those feelings
- Safe expression of the feeling
- Gaining support or sharing as a way to handle feelings, if required
- Sharing with other people thoughts about the feelings if they are involved
- Acknowledging the feelings of other people to whom you relate.

These steps may be difficult to manage. In practice feelings arise at any time as a result of conscious or subconscious thoughts. For example, a feeling of deep sadness which could involve expression through tears may in certain environments be regarded as inappropriate behaviour, such as in a work meeting. In this situation, looking after oneself may involve acknowledging the feeling of sadness and, at a more convenient time (e.g. later that day) reconnecting with the feeling and giving expression to it.

Sharing feelings with others may also be difficult, especially without allocating blame or criticism, or without feeling blamed or criticised by another person.

In emotional processing, any change (large or small) can be seen as triggering the thoughts and feelings described by the model in Figure 6.6, known as the 'transition curve' (Sugarman, 1986). Patterns of thoughts and feelings may vary from change to change, or person to person since the curve is simply a typical, temporal representation of these. For example, a person may 'miss out' one or two of the stages. Another common experience is to stall in one part of the curve, going over the same thoughts or feelings again and again. Eventually, after a period of time (which could be a matter of seconds or years) the transition will be completed.

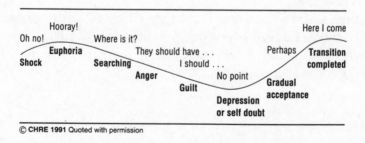

© CHRE 1991 Quoted with permission

Figure 6.6 Feelings about change: a pattern of transition

80

In identifying the feelings involved it is necessary to recognise that a change has occurred. It is understandable that sometimes change is resisted. Change is potentially frightening and stressful, an unsought necessity to explore an uncertain future, leaving behind the apparent safety of the familiar. In these circumstances the desire to hold on, to remain with the 'present', can be extremely strong. The difficulty with this is that the 'present' situation no longer exists as the change has already taken place or is about to.

This clinging to the past may be the holding on to something that no longer exists, as the individual seeks to retain the past as their current reality (Rogers, 1961). Within a certain period of time depending on individual processing, the support available, and the degree of physical and psychological discomfort (or 'dissonance', Festinger, 1957) the individual will have thought through the change and be looking ahead to some anticipated future.

There are a number of further ways of identifying and dealing with feelings; two will be considered here.

The first seeks to identify the thoughts which precede the feeling. Since all feelings arise from either conscious or subconscious thoughts it is possible to identify the thought which took place. This thought may be rational or irrational based on commonly held beliefs (Whycherley, 1986). In this way an individual may believe 'I should be liked by everyone'. This will probably create sadness or anger when they meet someone whom they perceive to dislike them. However the thought 'I should be liked by everyone' is irrational; a more rational thought may be 'I am liked by some people'.

The second approach involves acknowledging the feeling, respecting oneself, and then taking the feeling into a larger consciousness. This is done by asking questions such as 'What is behind this feeling?' 'Now what is behind that thought?' 'What is behind that?' and so on. (For a more detailed exploration see Levine, 1991). Transactional analysis also offers a similar exercise called 'trackdown', (Harris and Harris, 1985), which identifies the original feeling/ thought behind a train of thought.

Behavioural processing: ways of doing

Behavioural processing is best illustrated by the skills resources bank available to the individual, already described in Figure 6.1, which can enhance the ability to manage change and to function competently in a demanding world. In this analysis, skills refer to those which are more than trained physical/sensory/motor abilities such as driving, wood cutting, typing. These life skills are complex in nature and supported by knowledge, attitudes and beliefs. Such skills include decision-making, caring for oneself, negotiation, stress management and goal setting.

Ways of behaving are complex and often derive from habitual patterns. In order to extend skills, existing patterns (including ways of thinking, feeling and doing) need to be challenged, modified and relearned. This is needed so that newer, more appropriate and effective behaviours can be implemented by the individual. The view adopted here, and confirmed by those working in the area of life skills, is that new ways of behaving and acting can be adopted at any age, stage or time. Although the skills associated with managing change are usually learned incidentally without a conscious plan, it would seem that individuals can enhance their managing change abilities by further purposive learning and development.

This is supported by the experience of people themselves. For example, the opportunity to plan for mid-life or retirement involving reflection on and reference to the person's own experience and understanding, and then providing access to the development of additionally needed skills, will increase the ability of the individual to manage age-related life change (Phillipson and Strang, 1983; Riker and Myers, 1990; Coleman and Chiva, 1991).

Application of personal philosophy

The psychological benefits of having an identified personal philosophy are potentially numerous and can provide meaning and purpose for the individual. It also enables an image of the world to be constructed and maintained, and provides a framework in which the individual can operate with increased confidence and consonance (Festinger, 1957).

The shape of this philosophical framework can vary from person to person. A personal philosophy is based on understanding, beliefs, attitudes and values, to which the individual attaches specific meaning. Philosophical meanings appear initially to be culturally derived, as shown by the many different cultures across which the striving for meaning and purpose can be seen (Levine, 1991). Such striving for meaning; and rationalisation in a confusing and sometimes arbitrary, chaotic world is seen by many as a key aspect of 'being human' (e.g. Jung, 1967; Jarvis and Walters, 1993).

The notion of a philosophy of personal existence arising from a psychological need for a structure may in contrast seem functionalist and ontological. However, the striving of many people to rationalise or make meaning in their life is clear. The reasons for this striving may be those of consonance as Festinger suggests; or to create meaning as Kelly suggests; or shaping the world as Rogers suggests or ego transcendence as Erikson suggests; or as a fundamental element of human consciousness as Jung suggests. The need to establish meaning from wherever it arises is hard to deny.

The personal motivation involved in constructing a personal philosophy that fuels a striving after meaning can be quite strong and may increase as people reach mid and later life and a greater physical mortality is perceived. The shape of this sought-for philosophy is dependent on the way experience has been mediated by the individual, by the mechanism of framing and reframing of experiences, (Usher, 1989; Weil and McGill, 1989). The extent to which the philosophy is consciously derived is highly individual, depending on personal and social characteristics, such as the way personal power is perceived and used. The locus of this power may be internal or external. Personal philosophies can themselves also be internalised or externalised, or located in both domains in a combined way. The short analysis that follows is designed to portray the acquisition of a personal philosophy.

Ideas about personal philosophy may be internally or externally perceived or combinations of both. *Internally* located philosophy may include:

complete reliance on self, there being no other 'power',
personal skills / gifts
the fact of being alive / one's existence
the role or job

Externally located philosophy
the family
a partner
children
life, the fact of existence (outside oneself)
existence of natural patterns and beauty
a 'connectedness' to a power larger than oneself

Combined internally and externally located philosophy
a home
the work I do
personal cultural tradition
personal religious beliefs / spiritual understanding

In terms of managing change, the question could be asked concerning which philosophies may provide greatest support to the individual, but there would be no simple answer. Relative values would relate more to the quality of the belief, the degree of adherence to the principles of the belief; the way the philosophy is perceived to explain change and crisis in the individual's life; the desire to 'hide' within the belief from the perceived reality or demand of the changes, etc.

Personal philosophy provides a route map for guiding the individual through complex and conflicting norms and beliefs, within the self and others and society, and over time. As a guide, a personal philosophy itself will be called into question, reappraised in the light of experience and reformed. Its value lies in its applicability, its explanatory function, or its rationalisation function. In terms of psychological defence, the role of philosophy is obvious.

In terms of managing life changes the role of strongly held sets of beliefs can provide points of reference around which change in an individual's life can be orientated.

Summary

A functional review has taken place of the holistic self and the way that dynamic elements of the self interrelate to produce action in managing life change in the adult and older adult.

It has sought to portray the relationships between innate potential, the development process and maintenance processes. These aspects inter-relate to create a balance which can be positively shifted by further development of skills such as those factors which can help the individual to manage change (e.g. taking stock, understanding the change, managing the stress and seeing the change as more of a gain than a loss). If individuals plan for and develop life skills, coping with change will be facilitated. Many blocks and barriers can exist which inhibit change. These include resistance to acknowledging feelings associated with change; an incorrect perception of personal abilities with regard to the degree of demand in a situation, beliefs which are not supported by the realities of the situation; too many apparent conflicting changes; and the inability to manage stress.

Positively, it can be observed that human beings, irrespective of age strive to achieve balance and a higher level of being. The process of being and becoming remains both dynamic and holistic.

7 Development and personal growth: A personal reflection

Lorna Andrew

When I am an old woman I shall wear purple
With a red hat which doesn't go, and doesn't suit me.
And I shall spend my pension on brandy and summer gloves
And satin sandals, and say we've no money for butter.
I shall sit down on the pavement when I am tired
And gobble up samples in shops and press alarm bells
And run my stick along the public railings
And make up for the sobriety of my youth.
I shall go out in my slippers in the rain
And pick the flowers in other people's gardens
And learn to spit.

This excerpt is from *Warning* by Jenny Joseph (*Selected Poems*, Bloodaxe Books). The popularity of Jenny Joseph's poem confirms what Dr Johnson, describing a quite different experience, called 'the triumph of hope over experience' (1770). Wordsworth suggests a more realistic path of personality development towards old age, in *My Heart Leaps Up* (1807).

So it was when my life began;
So it is now I am a man;
So be it when I shall grow old,
Or let me die!
The Child is father of the Man;

Although we are constantly changing, both physically and mentally, throughout life, the emotional development of the person tends to become set more readily than that of body or mind. Peter Fletcher (1972), in his classic self-help work on emotional problems asserts that those carers responsible for children's upbringing ensure that their charges "reach physical maturity while remaining utterly dependent emotionally on the religious, moral, social and cultural judgements of their elders, and that they have pursued this aim to such good effect that fear of emotional freedom has become one of the most characteristic and pervasive motivations of contemporary civilisation." As we approach the third millennium we might like to think that this could no longer be true. It is more fashionable these days to speak of 'peer pressure'. But I am all too well aware that my own rigid Calvinist upbringing still influences me far more than the much more palatable ideas and lifestyles of my peers!

A secure base

The way in which we handle ourselves throughout life begins to be determined in infancy by the response of mother, or mother substitute, and subsequently by significant others (i.e. siblings, teachers, best friends, spouses, employers, even therapists). Donald Winnicott, a psychoanalyst who started his professional life as a paediatrician said in 1957, "There is no such thing as a baby", always "a nursing couple". John Bowlby (1980) believes that "Intimate attachments to other human beings are the hub around which a person's life revolves, not only when he is an infant or a toddler, or a school child, but throughout his adolescence and his years of maturity as well, and on into old age."

Sometimes these affectional bonds get disrupted and the child's secure base is lost or threatened. If the *together* person is the infant who was physically *held together* in his mother's arms, then any significant interruption of what Winnicott calls "good enough" parenting or holding can threaten that person' s sense of self (self-confidence, self-esteem, self-reliance). From this "good enough" parent the tiny child can learn a pattern or self-reliance resting on a secure attachment to a trusted figure. Bowlby (1979) describes some of the childhood experiences which often appear to lie behind anxiety, immaturity and over-dependence if these are present in later life:

- One or both parents may be persistently unresponsive, rejecting or disparaging of the child's pleas for affection and caring.
- Parenting is discontinued more or less frequently, and the child may spend time in hospitals or other institutions.
- Control is maintained by parental threats not to love the child.
- One parent threatens to abandon the family as a means of disciplining the child or coercing the spouse.

- One parent threatens to desert, or even kill the other, or to commit suicide.
- The parent induces the child to feel guilty by claiming that the child's behaviour will be responsible for the parent's illness or death. "You'll be the death of me!"

The death or loss of one or both parents speaks for itself, especially if it takes place before the age of conscious grieving.

Any of these experiences can lead a child, or adult, to live in constant anxiety lest he lose one of his significant attachment figures. The older person may be losing attachment figures one after another: The parents go; the children go; the career goes; colleagues, friends and relatives go; and often the partner or spouse goes. A well developed self-reliance is almost literally a life-saver. The annual suicide figures show that a significant number of elderly people take their own lives each year. In 1977-8 the peak suicide rate for men - well over 200 per million population - was attained by men aged over eighty. Overall, while in England and Wales the elderly comprise fifteen per cent of the population, they account for one third of the suicides. During the Cold War West Berlin, with its geographically isolated and generally ageing population, had one of the highest suicide rates. If, in assessing suicide risk, common factors to look for are age over forty-five, physical illness, social isolation, unemployment, bereavement and other losses, then older people must be considered potentially vulnerable.

Second chances

Erik Erikson (1950, reprinted 1963) developed a theory of psychosocial developmental stages which covers the life span. Each stage contains a conflict which has to be resolved, and the task of each stage is the resolution of this conflict. At any point in the life span *personality* is the product of the way in which these conflicts have been resolved.

STAGE	CONFLICT	RESOLUTION
1. Infancy	Trust vs. basic instinct	Hope
2. Toddler	Autonomy vs. shame and doubt	Will
3. Play age	Initiative vs. guilt	Purpose
4. School age	Industry vs. inferiority	Competence
5. Adolescence	Identity vs. role confusion	Fidelity
6. Young adulthood	Intimacy vs. isolation	Love
7. Maturity	Generativity vs. stagnation	Care
8. Old age	Integrity vs. despair	Wisdom

In the first stage (Freud's Oral stage) the infant's task is to learn that the mother may be trusted to return. In the second, (Freudian Anal) the task is to learn when it is appropriate to hold back and when to let go (will power). In the third, the child develops his conscience, hopefully without too much guilt attached. During the fourth and fifth stages the child/adolescent learns to win recognition by producing things and becoming competent. The first adult task is to establish an intimate relationship with another person, which involves having the confidence to lose part of the self in the merging with another. If this is achieved, such a relationship fosters creativity (stage seven), both in the sense of production, and of caring for the next generation. The task in the final stage is to review life's successes and failures, and to recognise it as continuing to be worthwhile, "the detached yet active concern with life in the face of death".

Erikson describes the eighth stage as that of "integrity vs. despair". Integrity can mean getting in touch with as yet unexpressed parts of the person. (Is this what Jenny Joseph's poem quoted at the beginning of the chapter is about?) It can mean getting back to parts long since lost touch with, because of the demands of career and parenthood. How many parents have become so accustomed to calling each other Mum and Dad that they never call each other Mary and Joe, even though the children have long since left home? It can mean knowing that we learn from all experiences, both good and bad. Jung (1993) would see it as meaning the enrichment, balance and completion which come in the second half of life.

How the "integrity vs. despair" scale tips will depend more on the way solutions have been reached to earlier crises and conflicts, than on current circumstances. To some people change will always be perceived as exciting and a challenge. To others change will be seen as frightening, a preview of the end.

Fortunately, life does give most of us second chances. Many of us will remember with gratitude, even affection, the interest, understanding and support of a particular teacher. Childhood playmates and their parents allowed others of us to glimpse the strength of lively and loving families. Some of us fall in love with the right person. Some of us have found our way to be respectful and trustworthy therapists. Some of us have labradors. And we retire.

Retirement and change

Retirement is still a relatively new phenomenon. Our great-grandparents probably did not retire at all. They lived shorter lives and worked longer. They had no pension funds, no National Health Service, no Social Security. We are still not sure what is the right age for retirement, or whether it should be the same age for men and for women. Retirement at sixty-five was set arbitrarily. Many of us think of ourselves as reaching our most productive period just when we are told that it is time to retire. Some of us are still thinking: "When I grow up, I'll be . . ." or "When we settle down, we'll . . ." or "When we get things sorted out, we'll . . ." even as we approach retirement. Retirement has been called "the first insult of ageing". But more people are retiring younger, by choice, semi-choice (retirement packages), or necessity (stress, ill-health, redundancy). A fifty year old worker, having left or lost his/her job will have difficulty selling him/herself on the job market.

The adjustment to retirement is one of the major adaptive tasks of later life, and the degree to which this adjustment is successful plays a major role in determining the extent to which individuals feel that their later years are satisfying and rewarding. Retirement is not just a simple change of status from the role of worker to that of non-worker; it has important interpersonal and intrapersonal implications which affect the person's total existence.

A job can provide security, activity, structure, identity, purpose, mastery, creativity, social interaction, even ritual. Retirement will not provide the same satisfactions, even though for many people it comes as a reward and a liberation. The income will be less, and the life style will usually change. For some people the loss of their job is a blow similar to the loss of a loved one. The grief process can be long and painful and frightening. Some retired people would seem to die of a broken heart within a short time of leaving their employment; the so called 'Sudden retirement death syndrome'.

Existing marriages will be different after retirement. The retired couple may be *full-time* husband and wife for the first time. A study carried out in Bristol within the last fifteen years showed that while thirty-five percent of wives looked forward to seeing more of their husbands, only fifteen percent of the husbands looked forward to more time with their wives. Retirement may be less threatening for women because our culture allows women to retire into domesticity thus providing a role. Increasingly, however future cohorts of retiring women may find this cultural expectation a less helpful feature of retirement. If it is the husband who is retiring from his job, does a non-working wife, retire too? Will she want him to participate in domestic arrangements and management? If a working wife continues in employment it can be hard to come home in the evening and find him already well settled into his pre-dinner drink, even worse with a friend or old colleague, and no third glass ready and waiting for the still-working partner. In retirement space and privacy are much harder to find.

Social interactions are different. There are not longer built-in colleagues for company. Some retired people circumvent this difficulty by congregating in the parts of the country well-known as retirement areas for particular professions, ie., Camberley or Cheltenham.

Retired people will be more dependent on family and friends. They will have something like two thousand more free hours each year to occupy. If there are few friends or no family, the potential for loneliness is great. And there is that ageing body to remind us of time left rather than time spent! Not so long ago I went into a jewellery shop to ask the price of a particularly fine pair of earrings. I came out empty-handed after thinking that it would not really be worth spending all that money considering the time I probably had left.

The attitude to retirement has more to do with feelings about ourselves than about the job we may be about to leave. Like leaving home, choosing a partner, having children, retirement can be one of the second chances of life. Everyone will experience emotions in coming to terms with so great a change after probably thirty or forty years of seeing ourselves as workers. Most people manage very well; but some people are more at risk than others.

The protestant work ethic is still powerful in our culture, even after year of high unemployment. Work brings self-esteem. No work can bring guilt, even sin. "The devil makes work for idle hands." Retirement is especially difficult for the *workaholic*, who may be just as addicted to his job as the alcoholic to his drink. Work is his fix, and no work means painful withdrawal symptoms. Workaholics often cope with the problems of retirement by becoming passionately attached to something taken up in retirement - golf or politics for example.

A job brings with it a certain status, and sense of identity. If this status has been overly important because the individual feels no sense of his own worth or identity, retirement can feel demeaning, and the retired person can feel worthless: The teacher with no class; the dentist with no drill; the soldier with no gun. The compulsive, obsessional man or women often needs the structure, not to say ritual of the job, and finds the loss of routine hard to accommodate. The ambitious goal-seeker finds few satisfaction to his liking in the more relaxed pattern of retired life.

For some people the job may have compensated for all the things which are not right elsewhere, especially in personal relationships. When the job goes they may have time and space to look at what has been going wrong - the repressed areas of their lives. And if this is really too frightening to do, some people might find themselves in the grip of psychosomatic illnesses.

Although attitudes towards retirement appear to have more to do with feelings about ourselves than with perceptions about our jobs, research carried out by Dan Jacobsen (1976a) suggest that the more rewarding and satisfying the job is perceived to be, the less the worker desires to retire. His studies show (1976b) that women are less likely than men to be positively oriented towards retirement. Only 41.4% of women, as against 62.1% of men preferred to retire at pensionable age.

"You may be old, but I am in my prime!"

How we perceive age and ageing is another factor in how we deal with our own and others' ageing. As a young person I thought of older age either in terms of TS Eliot's shrunken man:

I grow old . . . I grow old . .
I shall wear the bottoms of my trousers rolled.
> From *The love song of J. Alfred Prufock*

or in terms of Frances Cornford's dotty:

O fat white woman whom nobody loves,
Why do you walk through the fields in gloves . . .
Missing so much and so much?
> From *To a Fat Lady Seen from a Train*.

I find it hard to subscribe to my own advancing years, though I accept that memoranda will be taking the place of memory, and that climbing hills and jumping the streams in Scotland are no longer the fun they were. Perhaps all those working with older people should ask themselves questions like: "What is your *personal* experience of older people?", "How do you feel about getting old?", "Are you old?", "How old do you feel right now?", "Do you know why you feel that age?".

Our culture applauds those people who age well (who look young). The most prestigious magazines are full of advertisements for and articles about anti-ageing products. In one issue of the British *Vogue* (September 1994) there were twenty advertisements or articles specifically focused on ageing (anti-ageing), from the advertisement for "a unique non-surgical treatment for the ageing face" to the review of Erica Jong's latest book, *Fear of Fifty* (1994). Retirement is enthusiastically advertised as a leisure life-style, yet to describe someone as old is seen as an insult. All this implies that the pills and potions work, and that the money, albeit not quite so much, keeps rolling in, and that the friends are still around. In the end it may not quite work that way. Then, what really matters is how we have learned to cope with the emotional, physical and material changes as they come, for come they will. My grandparents had a hard and busy life bringing up ten children on a large Canadian farm. When they were dying, both in their late eighties, and both in great pain, they were moved downstairs to share a room, to make life easier for their carers. I was sixteen when I visited them for the last time, and my grandmother said to me: "Lorna, this has been my happiest year. Your grandfather and I have had time at last really to get to know one another."

PART III
Contexts for learning in an ageing society

8 The ageing self

Mike Hepworth

'Act your age!' is an admonition with which everyone is familiar. It is also one which raises important questions concerning the nature of the ageing process. How does one know how to act one's age? What is one's age? Is age determined by the number of years lived, by one's position in the life course? Is it determined by a biological clock, or by subjective experience - the way one feels about oneself? and in any case, what is the precise nature of the self?

Amidst the array of confusing and ambiguous questions surrounding ageing and old age two important issues are clear. The first is that the subjective experience of ageing, what we may describe as 'the ageing self', diverges, often quite dramatically, from the experience of the ageing body and the ways in which society categorises those who are chronologically older. As Paul Thompson (1992), for example, has shown, the phrase 'I Don't Feel Old' is frequently on the lips of men and women as they move into the chronological category of 'later life'.

The central issue here, he writes, is that "You may be categorised as an 'old person' with a pension and cheap travel concessions at 65, or according to medical and sociological specialists you may cross from the 'young old' to the 'old old' at 75, but there is no reason why you should not still feel the same person inside.'" (pp. 43-4). The heart of the matter is a tension between the physical processes of ageing especially as they are revealed in visible changes to the appearance of the body, and the inner or subjective sense of a 'real self' which often seems to be untouched by physical age. (Featherstone and Hepworth, 1989; Hepworth, 1991). In short, the visible body and the inner self do not appear to age simultaneously, and the ageing of the self is often perceived as qualitatively distinct from the ageing of body.

Indeed, the ageing of the body is often seen to pose a direct threat to the self. In his study of patients suffering from rheumatoid arthritis, Michael Bury (1982) shows that one of the non-medical consequences of this chronic illness is the disruption of the personal biography. As a chronic illness, rheumatoid arthritis threatens not only physical health and the well-being of the sufferer but is 'precisely that kind of experience where the structures of everyday life and the forms of knowledge which underpin them are disrupted.' (p. 169). As in the case of ageing, with which arthritis is often (wrongly) associated, a major issue for the patient is increasing dependency on others. One consequence of this awareness is a 'fundamental re-thinking of the person's biography and self-concept' (p. 169). A significant source of difficulty for patients who are younger is precisely the popular association of arthritis with age: a 'wear and tear disease' (p. 171). The stereotype of arthritis implies premature ageing and thus represents a shift from 'a perceived normal trajectory through relatively predictable chronological steps, to one fundamentally abnormal and inwardly damaging. The balance between internal and external reality is disturbed and the sufferer has become an ageing self, so to speak, before his or her time.

One of the most noticeable changes to have taken place in the structure of the life course during the period of modernisation is what Martin Kohli has described as 'chronologisation' (1986, p. 272). Life has become temporalised in such a way that each individual moves chronologically through 'sequences of positions' or 'careers' and 'biographical perspectives and actions' (1986, p. 273). The concept of linear time, as a controllable resource which determines the quality of life one has to live, has literally become the essence of life, and age-related categories, as Bury's research shows, determine expectations of the timing of the ageing process and the onset of what is believed to be old age. In his research into the attitudes of older Aberdonians towards illness and death, Rory Williams (1990) provides evidence of the hope of dying 'on time'. The men and women he interviewed, who were aged 60 and over, often expressed the belief in 'a natural time to die' (p. 93); an idea, he notes, 'directly connected with age, in the notion that one should die when old but not too old...' (p. 93). Here is evidence therefore, of a culturally prescribed balancing act between ideas of 'dying too soon' (p 95) and dying too old. The notion of 'your time' (p. 95) that is the timing of the death of the self was constructed out of a set of shared beliefs concerning the ideal death in old age. The 'doctrine of a natural term made prolonged survival unnatural, and dying young unjust...' (p. 98).

The second issue which stands out amongst the confusion surrounding the relationship between the ageing body and the ageing self is the central importance for the individual of maintaining the continuity of self in later life. In Rory Williams' research there are significant references to the ways in which a number of his interviewees would punctuate their accounts with 'self-characterisations', the most common being 'the theme of constant self'. (p. 290). The theme of a constant self was displayed in 'direct claims about what "I have always been" or "I have never been" and were frequently introduced by the phrases referring to qualities which were "part of me", "my own", or which "I am in myself"...' (p. 290). The significance of the concept of the self as a persistent object, was also demonstrated, for example, in Sharon Kaufman's (1986) systematic interviews with Californians aged 70 and over. Kaufman's key finding was that the men and women in her study did 'not perceive meaning in ageing itself; rather they perceived meaning in being themselves in old age.' (p. 6). She stresses that older people 'do not speak of being old as meaningful in itself, that is, they do not relate to ageing or chronological age as a category of experience or meaning. On the contrary, when old people talk about themselves, they express a sense of self that is ageless - an identity that maintains continuity despite the physical and social changes that come with old age' (p. 7).

At the beginning of this chapter attention was briefly drawn to the question of the nature of the self. In her research Kaufman defines the self as an 'interpreter of experience' (p. 14). Each individual make sense of experience within the framework provided by culture, utilising the resources which are historically available. As a consequence, when individuals come to deal with the 'physical and mental manifestations of old age' (p. 161), they continue their practices of a lifetime and struggle to 'maintain an ageless sense of self, therefore, the self is essentially ageless: the ageless self is 'the self employing the past as a resource for creating meaning in present encounters'. (p. 165). And, significantly for education for retirement, this takes place within a cultural context characterised by Kaufman as one with a predominant belief in the 'perfectibility of human existence through education, work, good deeds, and freedom of choice...' (p. 167).

The self as a life long process

In her analysis of the ageless quality of the self as an interpretive resource, Kaufman is indebted to the processual model of the self developed in America during the first quarter or so of this century by the philosopher and psychologist, George Herbert Mead, (Baldwin, 1986). The essential aspect of Mead's work for the understanding of the relationship between ageing and the self can be found in his opposition to the belief that the human self could be defined as something akin to a biological structure, and in his analysis of society and self a dynamically interacting processes. (Morris, 1991). Mead's work on the relationship of mind, self and society offers an alternative to the dualistic assumption that the body and the self exist on analytically separate levels and occupy different domains. For Mead the inner subjective world of the self is closely interrelated with the external social world of which it is inevitably a part.

For Mead the self is not present in the body at birth but originates in the dependency of the human infant on the mother and other carers. In this state of dependency the infant is incomplete and can only come into being as a self through the reciprocal communications with others in the social world outside. The infant will not survive unless other people, older and more socially sophisticated, respond to its primitive cries and gestures. In this respect the human species can be distinguished from animals because human beings, as social creatures, rely upon an infinitely more complex system of symbolic communication. For Mead the essence of self is meaning: the human capacity to create a complex repertoire of symbols and to recreate meaning continuously throughout a lifetime. Human beings, therefore, respond to each other on the basis of imaginative activity. And the core of imagination in the place of the other; to see one's self, so to speak, through their eyes. Thus the infant develops the ability to imagine the mother coming to stop the crying and can therefore begin to appreciate a distinction between the self and the other and to anticipate or mentally rehearse sequences of social interaction.

The self, therefore, is divided into two interdependent parts: the 'self' and the 'other'. From earliest infancy, awareness of self emerges with reference to awareness of the other, and the need to take the role of the other in order to establish the essential relationships of survival. Mead then adds a further elaboration. He divides the self into the 'I' and the 'Me'. The 'I' is that spontaneous aspect of the self which exists in the immediate, although fleeting present. The 'I' is the subject and the 'Me' the object, a kind of social conscience constructed out of the awareness from infancy of the attitudes and social expectations of others. The reciprocal relationship of the 'I' and the 'Me' is indicated in Mead's definition of the self as an internal conversation as reflected in the capacity of the individual to say: 'I said to myself...' The self is thus the human capacity to creatively develop language. As Sabat and Harré have observed in the study of the construction of self in Alzheimer's Disease (1992), the 'expression of complex acts of self monitoring' is made possible by the 'indexical structure' of language (p. 450). Even when there has been detectable organic damage to the brain the self as 'a personal singularity' (p. 444) continues to exist as long as an individual is able to publicly utter the word 'I'. According to their analysis senile dementia cannot destroy the self so long as the sufferer is able to symbolically refer to the self in conventional linguistic terms. In this analysis also the self is essentially ageless.

In Meadian analysis of the self the locus of reality is the present: the past is reconstructed and the future anticipated from the position of the present. As Chappell and Orback (1986) indicate, 'the elderly live in the present and remember their past, as do others, from the perspective of their present situations.' (p. 87). The old are not able to live in the past any more than the members of any other age group. 'The fact' they write, 'that change is inherent in the process of living, whether we are particularly aware of it or not, is important to remember in relation to the elderly, whose lives frequently are characterised as standing still. Not only is this characterisation false, but it also tends to keep us from recognising the potential of rich and full lives in old age.' (p. 88). Because the individual is always in a state of becoming, the continuous emergence of new situations requires continual reorganisation and reconstruction of the self.

The concept of selfhood as a continuous process that can only come to an end with death has much to offer the social construction of positive ageing. If it is accepted that the self is essentially a dynamic social process, created and sustained through social interaction and communication, then ageing takes on a new meaning in a society where the majority of older people are not significantly mentally or physically impaired. And even when mental impairment exists, the interactionist approach to the self is increasingly being seen as a constituting a sound basis for remedial intervention and dignified care (Kitwood, 1990; Sabat and Harré, 1992).

If we return to the questions with which this chapter opened, we can pose the additional question: what kind of ageing self do we wish for ourselves and for others? Mead teaches us that as experiences accumulate, the range of resources open to each individual changes and modifies the relationship (both in terms of quality) between the past, the present (where, he argued, all individuals are inescapably situated) and the future. Although the reality of the ageing body and the finitude of human life cannot ultimately be denied, there is sufficient evidence from both research and everyday experience to suggest that the most effective prescriptions for 'positive ageing' in the future will focus on reflexive control over the social resources that constitute the ageing self.

One source of optimism is the championship of the notion of life as a spiritual journey (Cole, 1992) - or at least of older age as an enrichment of the self - by the increasingly influential school of humanistic gerontologists. Sally Gadow (1986), for example, now speaks of the possibility of enriching the meanings given to frailty by transforming it from an enemy of the self into a 'source of intensity and life without which no self is whole'. (p. 243). For Gadow 'Decay and weakness are manifest not in the body's decline, but in the lack of vitality in the self to embrace one's life, including the life of the body with its unceasing tides of strength and frailty.' (p. 241).

9 Being and learning in the late twentieth century

Peter Jarvis

For when I was a babe and wept and slept,
Time crept;
When I was a boy and laughed and talked,
Time walked;
Then when the years saw me a man,
Time ran;
But as older I grew,
Time flew

(Epitaph - Chester Cathedral)

This beautiful epitaph captures a phenomenon with which most people are familiar, the subjectivity of our experience of time. Time no longer seems static, it appears to be flowing more quickly as every day passes - time speeds up as we age. But the world in which we live in the late twentieth century in Western Europe is also one in which we are becoming increasingly aware of transience. Bauman (1992) epitomises this experience thus:

> Nothing can be done forever. Knowledge that I studiously master today will become thoroughly inadequate, if not downright ignorance, tomorrow. The skills I learn today by the sweat of my brow will not carry me far in the brave new world of tomorrow's technology. The job I won yesterday in fierce competition will disappear tomorrow. The career whose steps I am carefully negotiating will vanish - the stairs, the staircase, the building and all my prize possessions, my today's pride will tomorrow become yesterday's taste and my embarrassment (pp. 169-70).

It is, then, not only our perception of a more rapidly passing time as we age, we do actually live in a world in which everything is changing and the pace increasing. We are constantly made aware of the passage and speed of time passing. It is easy to feel that we are not keeping abreast with all the changes, that as we grow older we become obsolete in a world that is being transformed so rapidly. We become increasingly aware of how much we need to learn in order to feel at home in this transient world.

Immanuel Kant (1993 edn.) opened his *Critique of Pure Reason* by claiming that there can be no doubt that all our knowledge begins with experience. This is certainly true for learning, as the process through which we transform our experiences of the world and people into knowledge, skills, attitudes, and values, thus making them 'our own'. We subjectify this apparently objective and fast changing world and not only try to make sense of it, but also enable ourselves to function within it. Learning is crucial to our understanding of being, since it is an existential phenomenon. It is the process through which we become ourselves and for as long as our mental capacities remain unimpaired, we are able to learn, grow and develop.

But because the world is changing rapidly and we are ageing, our experiences of the physical and social world are frequently new ones, only some of which will our previous learning have equipped us to deal. Where this is the case, there is a kind of congruence, or harmony, between our biography and our experience and we have no need to learn anything. We can take the experience for granted and act unthinkingly, not even be aware of the passing of time. We often say that we act instinctively on these occasions although it is more accurately 'unconscious' because of previous learning. But the content of much of our experience of this world is not contained in our previous biography, and so there is a disjuncture between the biography and the experience and we need to learn from such perceptions (experiences) in order to continue to feel at home in the world.

However, we all have experiences of the modern world that are so far removed from our previous experiences that we are forced to admit that we feel estranged and cannot understand what is happening. In this technological world many of our experiences are mediated, or secondary. We read the newspaper, listen to the radio and watch the television and we experience a foreign world, often one which we have never visited. We thus have second-hand experiences of unusual situations, even by this world's standards, as if they were ordinary and everyday. No wonder the world sometimes seems a long way from our own lives, and our experiences appear to be far removed from our biographies.

For the sake of convenience we will call these three relationships between biography and experience: congruence, disjuncture and divergence. They can be depicted in the following diagram.

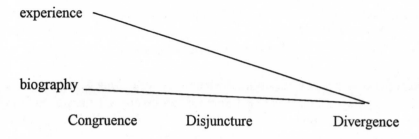

Figure 9.1 The relationship between biography and experience

These three relationships will now be explored in greater detail and, for reasons that will become more obvious as we proceed, the discussion will occur in reverse order.

Part 1 Divergence

In the changing world of late modernity in the West, where conditions change as rapidly as Bauman has suggested, it is not difficult to recognise how easy it is for our experience of the world to be widely divergent from our biography. We have no doubt all experienced situations in which this gap has been so great that we have had to admit we were rather like a fish out of water, and have needed help in order to understand the situation.

Modernity began with the Renaissance, in which new scientific ideas replaced the traditional order. Science and industrialism gradually emerged and with them the world of technological capitalism and instrumental rationalism. This is a world of new ideas and new inventions, where innovation is the order of the day and frequently even the things of yesterday are dismissed as traditional and out-of-date. It is a complex world where abstract systems have replaced individuals and these systems require a number of experts to service them. Change is not only rapid but it occurs throughout the whole of society. Even where the change is actually outside of our immediate focus of attention, as mentioned earlier, it is frequently communicated to us through the media, so that much of our understanding of the world is not through direct or first hand, experience but through secondary or mediated, experiences.

It is impossible to keep abreast with everything that is occurring. We may have to learn to accept the changes and trust the systems. Even when we want to understand new situations, this is prevented by their complexity. But this often leaves us feeling exposed and, consequently, isolated and ignorant amidst the sea of change. Giddens (1990, p.7) describes the nature of this modern society as ambiguous, since having a sense of security is always coupled with the realisation that this is a dangerous world, and trusting the systems is always tinged with the sense of having to take a risk. This is the world which Beck (1992) depicted as 'risk society'.

The experience of 'anomie' describes the feeling of wondering what this world is coming to, feeling a stranger within it. Some situations are so far removed from our experience that we cannot learn from them, except to recognise that we need to be taught. It is not surprising, therefore, that some people feel that they have to disengage from this world and seek harmony with their environment; they have been called the harmony seekers (Jarvis, 1992) who endeavour to create a restricted and stable socio-cultural environment with which they are familiar. Although this is something that some older people seek to do, we have to recognise that this is not only a feature of later life. Many people fear the freedom offered by this rapidly changing world (Fromm, 1942). But not all of our experiences are so divorced from our experiences and with others we have a sense of disjuncture, rather than complete divergence.

Part 2 Disjuncture

The diagram shows that there are a middle range of situations where our biographies are not totally in harmony with our experiences - these are labelled as disjunctural. Disjuncture occurs where we are sufficiently familiar with the situation for it to be meaningful but when we see that we do not have all the knowledge, skills, attitudes, etc. necessary to cope with it in a taken-for-granted manner. In other words, we are experiencing a novel situation and we have to learn something new in order to cope with it and to try to reach that state of harmony with our environment. The experience of disjuncture, then, is the beginning of our learning process, and it can be induced by changing situations, by other people (such as teachers or others who have themselves undergone change as a result of learning experiences since we met them last, etc.), or even by ourselves if we wonder why something that we have experienced has actually occurred.

Learning then begins with experience and while we may always be trying to re-establish harmony with our world so that we have the necessary understanding. to manage our experiences, we experience the world as something which keeps on changing, so that we keep on experiencing disjuncture with it. For as long as change lasts, for as long as we exist in time, we will continue to experience disjuncture. This is the modern order, which demands that people keep on learning new things in order to retain familiarity with it.

Learning is the process of transforming experiences of disjuncture with the

104

external world and internalising the outcomes into a part of our meaningful biography. By so doing we are constructing our own biography and becoming more experienced. There is a certain paradox here - that by being aware that we cannot cope with a situation we can set in train a process by which we learn to manage. In other words, we grow and develop because we respond to the gap between our experience and our biography by learning. Learning is the process through which we 'become', and we keep on becoming for as long as we continue to learn. The risk society is itself paradoxical since it generates situations which we cannot control, but they are also the very situations through which we learn and develop our own humanity. Learning is the very force of human development.

The question could be raised about why we feel that we have to keep abreast with all these changes and then we come back to the explanation that we do not like to feel strangers in the world. We need to be in harmony with our environment. Learning, then, seems to orientate us in the direction of congruence with our world, but the world is changing so rapidly that congruence is rather like a mirage. When we answer one question, another appears in need of a response, etc. Our disjuncture is not only between our biography and our experience, we experience it as a separation between us and our world and may wish that we could take this world for granted.

Part 3 Convergence

There are many situations in which our biographies and experiences converge. We can take them for granted and act in an almost unthinking manner. For as long as our taken for granted knowledge or skill etc. actually works we can continue in this way. In other words, as Heller (1984) argues, much of our everyday living is based upon pragmatism. We are in harmony with our environment and can act in the almost instinctive manner described earlier.

Indeed social living itself would be impossible unless there was congruence and no need to learn in every situation. When we speak, we assume that others can understand us; when we engage in social interaction of almost any form we assume that those with whom we act understand what is happening. We feel at home in this type of situation; we can cope in an unthinking manner. Consequently, it is hardly surprising that many people endeavour to create a social environment where they are not constantly forced to learn new things and trust abstract and complex systems.

Congruence, then, is a situation where little or no learning need occur before individuals can cope with situations that they experience. It is a security which is sought by many, even though they learn little new about the rapidly changing socioeconomic and technological world around them and may grow further apart from it - estranged from it in a sense, and be heard to say 'I don't know what this world is coming to these days'.

But there are others who are forced into situations which are themselves unchanging, among whom are older people who are in hospital or residential care. They may have no choice but to endure an unchanging situation, one in which there is monotonous routine and few stimulations introduced to create novelty. In such situations, they cannot learn even if they wanted to do so. Often because of shortage of staff or because of lack of training of staff, elderly people are placed in caring situations where they are given little or no opportunity to learn and then slowly they forget things that they have learned and used in other past situations. They become alienated because they know that they can neither change their environment, nor can they grow or develop in situations where they cannot learn and draw on the force of human development.

It is then assumed, if older people lose some of their mental faculties, that this is part of a natural unidirectional process of ageing. (But see Glendenning and Stuart-Hamilton, 1995, this series). We perceive that we tend to forget things as we age and so this assumption seems quite justified. However, older people, given the right conditions, can and do still retain many of their faculties and learn new things, and can even re-learn old things that they have forgotten as a result of a period of institutionalisation. However, this does take time and skill: the former, above all, is often lacking in the rapidly moving and so-called cost-efficient society; and the latter skills are similar to those of a teacher of younger children and there seem to be insufficient trained personnel either within the institutions or beyond them to effect this learning process successfully.

The situation of congruence, then, is itself paradoxical: it is one in which people can feel safe because they do not have to encounter the uncertainties of this rapidly changing world, but it is also one which can be destructive because it does not enable people to use their learning and so they forget what they have actually learned and used in the past.

Conclusion

In this rapidly changing world, one which some scholars regard as post-modernity (Lyotard, 1974) and others as late modernity, we all face a world in which all three forms of relationship between biography and experience exist. We all need the situation of congruence so that social intercourse at every level can occur; we also need and experience novel situations from which we can learn and grow and develop (and in contemporary society we have considerable choice about what we learn and how we develop); we also all experience divergence since the world is changing so rapidly and fragmenting as new specialist systems are introduced. For most people, it is a world of two sides as Giddens (1990, p.7) suggests: security versus danger and risk versus trust. It is double-edged, glorious but frightening.

But we are facing a major problem in the West. We are living longer and the world is changing more rapidly than ever before. It is one in which it is more easy to opt out of the risk society and to seek a more convergent situation as the gap between individuals and their world grows. It becomes increasingly easy, therefore, to regard later life as obsolescent and elders as people who have nothing more to contribute to this modern world, and so they tend to become even more isolated and may even be placed in care - care for their physical bodies but sometimes at the risk of mental neglect.

Whether in care or not, older people's apparent obsolescence is assumed because we tend to judge this modern world by the very symbols of modernity - instrumentality, technology, individuality and possessions. Elders exhibit many of the characteristics which are the antithesis of modernity - few need to be instrumental, many do not understand contemporary technology, but they do need relationships and they are not always seeking new possessions. In a sense they remain a symbol of our traditional humanity, with rich biographies and a wealth of experience which can be shared if opportunity is created to listen and learn. Continuing interaction between people of all ages is an enriching and necessary experience for Western society of the late twentieth century.

10 Disadvantage in later life: Information and educational needs

Mary Davies

Despite many newspaper and magazine articles which give the impression that life in retirement is about exotic holidays, where to invest sums of money etc. the reality for large numbers of people is very different. Many people are disadvantaged in later life, in fact, one way or another, nearly half of the population could be said to be disadvantaged in terms of their life situation. The disadvantages which can affect people in relation to retirement are listed in Table 10.1. Some people will clearly be in more than one of the groups.

Table 10.1
Disadvantage in later life groupings

- People who are disabled or retiring with chronic ill health.
- Women, particularly those who are single, divorced or widowed.
- People on low income with no occupational pensions.
- Black and ethnic minorities.
- Unpaid carers.
- People retiring from specific occupations which cause special difficulties e.g. loss of tied accommodation, compulsory relocation.

The disadvantaged in these groups may suffer multiple deficits, which result in relatively disempowered people who find it difficult to gain access to help and information. The final report of the Carnegie Inquiry into the Third Age (which summarised the nine independent reports it had commissioned), identified the issue of multiple disadvantage as a significant factor in the lives of a substantial minority of third agers. Those who had experienced poor education and training, low paid jobs, periods of unemployment or sickness or all of these, also faced poor prospects in retirement, the Inquiry concluded. Particularly badly off were the long-term unemployed in their 50s and those socially classified D and E who tended to live in rented accommodation and so were without the asset of a house or much flexibility to move. Such people were also less likely to have a car or good access to local shops and amenities (whether in rural or urban settings). Health status and expectation of life were lower, as was involvement in leisure or volunteer activities. Although the majority of third agers avoid such multiple disadvantage, and maintain or even improve their situations, the position of the least well off was identified by the Inquiry as one of its most important issues of concern.

The information equation

There are circumstances in later life which trigger a search or need for information or educational opportunity. One highly significant trigger is retirement, which can act as a prompt for several reasons. The retiree may need specific information about financial matters or the 2,000 extra hours each year at his or her disposal in the absence of work (which has been previously mentioned by Andrew, this volume). If this increased need for information and education can be met, then positive outcomes may result.

If in later life, circumstances diminish the capacity to obtain and cope with information and education, then there is an *information deficit* and the individual concerned is further disadvantaged. For various reasons all the disadvantaged groups listed earlier may find themselves having to cope with an information deficit. Another important factor is the way that information and education are supplied. For example, if the information or educational opportunity is offered in a way which patronises the consumer, there will be little demand for it. There are many other barriers to information/education which contribute to the information deficit.

Disadvantage in later life will now be discussed under the groupings suggested above.

People disadvantaged by chronic ill health or disability

According to a survey carried out by Eric Midwinter for British Gas (1991) being old did not mean being ill. Nevertheless 30 per cent of the people surveyed had some mobility problems and 24 per cent had other problems such as asthma

110

or heart problems.

In recent figures from a survey commissioned by the Department of Social Security ill health was shown to be a major factor in early retirement. More than 37 per cent of the retired men and 29 per cent of the retired women in their survey reported their own ill health as the main reason for taking early retirement.

Arber and Ginn (1991) devised a measure of functional disability (to do with capacity for everyday tasks, rather than reported illness) and concluded that older women (65+) are more likely to be substantially disabled than their male counterparts, with twice as many experiencing severe restrictions. Moreover, the level of difficulty increases with age for both women and men, along with the need for assistance.

Inequalities in health continue into later life (Victor, 1991) and older people from non-professional backgrounds consume hospital and GP services less than people from professional backgrounds. Morbidity and mortality are still demonstrably class related. Deteriorating health is an important key to information problems in later life, since ill health prompts a need for services and care as well as other non-medical information on how to obtain benefits and other means of support. Being chronically ill or disabled makes it much less likely that participation in educational opportunities will be achieved. Education centres may be difficult to get to, poor eyesight or hearing create further difficulties unless centres are prepared for such clients.

Many older people would prefer not to be out alone especially at night. The Carnegie report suggests that there may be a sub group of the population whose need for information and education remains unmet due to their lack of capacity to obtain it, because there are many in the third age who, whilst still active and independent, need social support of various kinds to help with mobility, sight, hearing and living alone. People who have become disabled as younger adults also face extra difficulties when older.

Women in later life: the gender disadvantage

Most married women currently entering retirement rely on the contribution records of their husbands for their pension rather than earning benefits in their own right. Since divorced women have no statutory right to a share of their ex-husband's occupational pension, many of them have nothing except the basic state pension which is also based on the ex-husband's National Insurance contributions. More than a third of marriages end in divorce and it has been predicted that by early next century one woman in six over the age of 60 will be divorced. Too few of these will have a pension unless younger women of today take action.

111

Although the law states that ex-wives should be compensated for lost pension rights, the courts have wide discretion and in practice it may not happen. Recent pension legislation has tried to address this overdue issue, which has no easy administrative solution. Single women in later life may also be financially less well provided for than men. They have often been in less well paid jobs, many without occupational pension schemes especially if employment has been part-time during periods of their lives when caring for younger or older family members. Third and fourth age women are more at risk of poverty than men.

Financial status may have some bearing on taking advantage of educational opportunities. Even if these are provided at low cost, there is still the cost of books, travel, coffee breaks and appropriate equipment in some instances. Leisure learning and, in some cases, vocational training now demand higher fees, following the changes in provision of further and adult education in 1992

There are other issues which disadvantage women. Sontag (1978) described female ageing as a negative and disempowering experience pointing out that society offers even fewer rewards for ageing women than it does for men. Feeling disempowered is not the best place to start from when faced with the need to obtain information, and probably means a lower likelihood of seeking access to educational opportunity.

Even the educational opportunity of pre-retirement preparation is less available to women who work for small firms or part-time.

Many older women live alone as shown in Table 1. (Diag. 8 p.5, Rapid Reports) and are more at risk of isolation.

In each group, the percentage of older women living alone is at least twice as high as that of men. This is due to the differences in life expectancy of men and women as well as differences in family situation. More than half of women in the 75-79 age group live alone. This may increase the need for educational opportunities, which are often also social opportunities. The informal transmission of information which relies on a social network may also be less available to people living alone unless the neighbourhood is a close community.

Many women living alone have no access to a car and should public transport be available fear, especially at night, may keep them from venturing abroad. These and other practical difficulties were described by the Carnegie Inquiry Reports on Education and Training, and on Leisure. Furthermore, much information exchange and learning goes on wherever people are gathered together informally such as pubs, clubs and cafes. It is not comfortable for older women to visit such places alone in the way that older men can. Perhaps this explains why such older women as do venture out are the mainstay of many evening classes and University of the Third Age (U3A) groups. Despite this many older women are experiencing an information/education deficit where their need has increased but, perhaps because of change in their lives, their capacity to obtain the education has meanwhile decreased.

The poverty disadvantage

In a recent Eurobarometer Report (1993), when the general public were asked an open-ended question about the main problems facing older people, the most frequently mentioned was financial problems, with an average of just under half of EC citizens saying that they regarded this as the main problem facing older people in their country.

The Carnegie Inquiry study on income reported that as a proportion of all income, earnings dropped sharply as a source within the third age period, as state-derived income became the greater source. Income from all sources continued to fall with age. Single women were the worst off group. Some 40 per cent of third agers had private pensions, but the majority of this group received low amounts. Private income of all kinds was very unevenly distributed. Factors producing poverty were unemployment and dependence on state benefits / pensions. Relative affluence depended on higher private pensions, younger age, but without dependents, home ownership and significant investment income. The overall distribution of income in the third age is similar to that of the whole population, supporting the concept of the transmission of disadvantage.

However, the majority see themselves as able to get by if they are careful. The UK results in the Eurobarometer table are more optimistic than the survey commissioned by British Gas in 1991 which reported that 31 per cent had to struggle to pay for necessities and 19 per cent even had problems keeping warm.

These differences illustrate the apparent paradox whereby older people who, by objective criteria, are suffering poverty and deprivation may nonetheless express subjective, satisfaction with their living standards. What effect is this likely to have on the educational opportunities of older people?

As mentioned earlier with regard to women's participation, formalised educational opportunities are seldom free. Recent changes in the UK in the way the Government funds adult education has had the effect of raising the costs of many courses, even those attended by retired people. Although concessions are sometimes available, books and other materials have to be obtained and the venue reached. Much educational opportunity is now available at home because of videos, home computers and television. So much of this opportunity is out of reach of people disadvantaged by poverty. As many of the poor in later life have been poor at all stages in life and in addition have had little opportunity for post-school education. The retired who most benefit from educational holiday tours, language teaching videos, expensive books about culture, are mainly those who have taken advantage of educational opportunities throughout their lives. In all studies of educational participation in later life, it is those who have already experienced post-compulsory learning who come back for more - an experience which is still class related.

One area where less well off people can obtain education is through television and radio. According to the Eurobarometer of senior citizens in the EC only one in three had read a book in the previous week. So the UK free library system may only benefit up to a third of older people. Several surveys, including that by British Gas, show that many retired people spend a great deal of their time watching television. This was the 'activity' undertaken by the largest number of them in the previous week according to the Eurobarometer survey, and also in the Carnegie Inquiry study on Leisure.

There are, however, some disadvantages in television as an educational medium. It mostly encourages a passive form of learning, where the learner cannot effectively challenge or elucidate the material with the result that what appears to be educational and informative could be misleading and misinforming. This disadvantage could be overcome if people watched television with others, then took some time together for discussion after the programme. Even a television and its licence have to be paid for and, for those who can only get by if they are careful, the cost may yet be too great.

Black and ethnic minorities

In the UK many black and minority ethnic retired people are poor, as they have been working in less well-paid jobs, often within their own families, and have suffered more unemployment so they are already disadvantaged by poverty. Many men are being made redundant / early retired from the declining manufacturing industries. They frequently do not qualify for full basic state pension or occupational pension, and many older women have not done paid work. The Carnegie Inquiry (1993) reported that its small sub-survey of ethnic minority elders showed a wish for language and other kinds of tuition and information but opportunities were not known and racial discrimination was feared. For educational opportunities to be acceptable, a cultural understanding is required by those who offer and deliver the service and, for some purposes, in the appropriate language. It is very easy, in ignorance, to offer the values of other cultures.

As far as pre-retirement education is concerned many black and minority ethnic people have worked in situations where there is no opportunity to go on a course or even know that such courses exist. This is noted in the British Gas report which

114

showed that there was substantially less planning for retirement by black and Asian older people.

According to Blakemore and Boneham (1994) two sets of factors shape the ageing of black and Asian peoples in Britain; first their own expectation of ageing and second the relationship between the minority community and the majority. The decision as to whether or not to maintain a distinctive ethnic identity will affect whether people seek out educational opportunities if they are not provided by their own ethnic group.

The racism still prevalent in the UK, and the fear of it, keeps many people locked up in the safety of their own communities and may be an additional barrier to educational participation. The term 'triple jeopardy' is often used: black, old and poor. Despite the strengths of family ties and community self-help, older people from black and Asian ethnic backgrounds are at risk of poverty and isolation, and can be shocked at the lack of status, role and respect showed to elders in the UK.

Providing educational opportunities in these situations needs to be done in partnership with members of the black and minority ethnic communities, or by offering the initial stimulus or resource if required so that they can provide it for themselves.

Unpaid carers

In the UK there are at least six million unpaid carers. The peak age for caring is 45 to 64 years, however, 42 per cent are over 60 years of age. Both men and women are carers, although the number of women involved is greater than that of men (Green, 1985). Women are also looking after more heavily dependent people and for longer hours; men are more likely looking after spouses. For carers the freedom of the third age may never happen. They are at risk of short and longer term poverty, especially if they do not have a job.

The caring role is usually undertaken in a family context (Jones and Vetter, 1984), and since extended family support has all but disappeared, the cost to the carer can be enormous leading to physical (health) emotional, social and financial difficulties. Many older carers are themselves in poor health, having to cope with considerable stress without social contact or holidays for example. In research carried out by the MSD Foundation (Davies, 1989), carers who were invited to participate in workshops commented that they were pleased to have an evening out "with a clear conscience".

How can people in this situation take advantage of educational opportunities? People who retire early to look after relatives may be offered pre-retirement education. Since only a small proportion of all retiring people are given this chance we can be sure that many people have not even been offered any opportunity to prepare. Carers are often reluctant to leave their relative at home alone, so unless there is some support the carer will be too anxious and guilty to go out.

The caring role itself creates a great need for information and education. For instance, carers need to find out what benefits are available, what social and medical support can be obtained, how to obtain counselling support, or how to set up a support group with other carers. It is a demanding role and does not leave much time, energy or enthusiasm for anything else. So how can carers gain access to educational opportunity?

To be able to attend classes on a regular basis requires a regular helper to free the carer. These are not easy to find, the person has to be acceptable to the carer and the relative. It may be easier to attend a Summer School or a weekend event on a one-off basis, since respite care may be a possibility freeing the carer for a specific amount of time.

For most people to be able to study, they require peace and quiet and to be able to free their mind at least for a while, so that they can concentrate. This would be difficult for many carers. Carers thus suffer from a double information/education deficit, in their caring role on behalf of their dependant, and also on their own personal account. This lack seems unjust when it is particularly remembered that their unpaid work saves the taxpayer millions of pounds a year.

People retiring from specific occupations

There are some occupations where retirement creates particular disadvantages for the individuals and their families. Large numbers of people have recently retired from the armed services where they have been provided with housing, schooling and medical services as part of their job. Not only do they have to cope with managing the usual changes in retirement, they also have to cope with a totally new way of life - possibly in a different country or a different part of the country. Access to educational opportunities in these situations were generally available through the armed services themselves and individuals have little direct experience of what is available to them or how they can obtain it. The advantage of a long professional life in the services is that individuals are likely to have regularly attended updating courses and training and therefore have life long experience of continuing education.

People in special occupations usually retire early and often have been aware of their retirement date for many years. They may also wish or need to find another paid job to supplement their pension. This may give them an added incentive to seek out learning opportunities. As made clear in the Carnegie Inquiry there are

116

at least two distinct groups in those people aged 50+ seeking education. There are those who are retired from paid work altogether and looking for general interest courses, and those who wish to find a further job after taking a vocational course. In the second category, career reorientation may not be an easy task for people who have been in the same job or work community for many years, particularly where work has been extremely specialised, or has relied on the individual's personality or style, or has involved a particular way of life. (some roles are particularly hard to relinquish, e.g. priest, police officer, public servant)

Conclusions

There are large numbers of older people who are disadvantaged in one or more ways so that they are unable to take advantage of learning opportunities. The lack of resources and opportunities in the third age have their causal root in the second, or even first, age. In the Carnegie Inquiry Report on Learning it was estimated that about three-quarters of a million people in the third age enrol annually in some kind of formal adult education and a similar number receive some kind of organised training. This means that only 1 in 10 of people over 50 take part each year in formal learning, yet policies on education and training, as well as leisure, transport, community care etc. ned to specifically recognise and combat disadvantage.

The barriers faced by disadvantaged people obtaining access to continuing education are summarised below, and are similar to those reported by Schuller and Bostyn (1992).

- Physical barriers such as getting to the education centre
- Financial barriers - paying for the education or books or residential accommodation and for transport
- Emotional barriers - anxiety about going out in the evening, or resuming learning after many years
- Attitudinal barriers - on behalf of the educator and the learner about education
- Lack of time - particularly for people in a caring role.

Overcoming the barriers

The barriers can be divided into internal and external barriers. The internal barriers the emotional and attitudinal ones, can only be overcome by the individual, though often requiring external stimulus or support. Older people need

117

to feel empowered to take advantage of and insist on their access to educational opportunities and to see themselves as active important members of society. The problem has a class dimension as already noted. In a survey carried out by MORI and commissioned by the National Institute for Adult and Continuing Education (NIACE)(1993), middle class adults are more likely to study later in life if they originally stayed on in education after the age of 18. It is likely that when people have become used to learning they feel comfortable with it and are keen to go on.

The external barriers need to be addressed at a policy level. Who should pay for the education, and what form it should take are key questions in this much needed policy debate. In the MORI/NIACE survey it was agreed by participants that the taxpayer should bear less of the cost and that individuals and employers should bear more. This would create higher barriers for many older people already disadvantaged by poverty. However, there are examples of education for older adults which are very cost effective. The University of the Third Age (U3A) is a good example of mutual self-help education (Midwinter, 1984). One of the ways forward may be for older people to do as in the U3A and use the skills and expertise of other older people which they give freely and generously. The disadvantage of this is that the provision is patchy. There are many benefits in this self-help approach for older adults in general, and examples can be found of self-help and mutual empowerment through which disadvantaged groups have benefited (see, for example, Chapter 12).

As Withnall and Percy (1994) point out when older people take responsibility in this way their collective significance is acknowledged and they offer new models of co-operative organisation to younger generations.

Carnegie identified outdated attitudes and practical barriers (based on an outmoded view of the later part of the life course) that still allowed third agers to cut themselves off, or to be cut off by others, from social involvement. Whilst individual older people have a responsibility for creating a rewarding retirement for themselves, and contributing to society as they are able, there are also many ways in which Government, organisations, service providers, employers, etc. could help. There is still a resistance to the change in attitude towards, and empowering of, older people that needs to happen. Their aspirations, and those of us all, for later life need to be better understood and catered for. New forms of participation, beyond current expectation, need to be facilitated, requiring the significant reduction of disadvantage as a priority.

11 Education for an ageing society

Joanna Walker

The ageing of all societies, even of the less industrialised ones, is a phenomenon that has existed long enough for the scale of the challenge to be grasped, but not yet long enough to have clarified the vision for future policy and action. We understand that the institutions of the latter half of the twentieth century, such as the welfare state, occupational pensions, careers followed by predictable retirement, were mature responses to the prevailing conditions of the times. Radical reform of these, driven by policy and by social and economic change, seems inevitable and contributes greatly to a current sense of insecurity and identity confusion in people of all ages, not just older people.

Productivity: a new paradigm?

Blaikie (1992) comments on the "spiritual and societal rethinking" that is entailed by the extent and nature of life after paid work if we are to negotiate an appropriate response to societal ageing. He likens this to a previous recognition of the part played by values (e.g. Protestantism) in the pervasiveness of work as a life structure. What values can support lives that are no longer so structured, and is age actually relevant to such a question? Will older age still imply a relinquishing of obligation to earn one's financial support? In the same way as disability and (single) parenthood are becoming less viable as non-obligated statuses, will 'productive ageing' emerge as a rationale for 'fourth age' retirement only? Will age-related work exit, reflecting labour market conditions, grow ever distant in time from retirement as defined by entry into public pension support, for those eligible?

Will there then be a group for whom public support is not available (because of income levels) whose age-related work exit is largely a matter of personal and financial choice and for whom, therefore, 'retirement' as a public or socially-sanctioned status is irrelevant? Would such a sub-group of the older population be likely to be more or less interested in participating in social life? Freed (or barred) from the opportunity to draw on the intergenerational social contract, at least until their fourth age, how would they see their third-age contribution?

Laslett's vision of personal fulfilment and the 'prime of life' quality of the post-work period was balanced by a requirement to act as cultural stewards for following generations. Much of the attractiveness and success of intergenerational educational work, popular in this decade, has been premised on the continuing interest and good-will of older people. Such engagement may revert to the sphere of private philanthropy, an obligation based not so much on 'noblesse' but on high material security.

What, then, of the not-so-secure, but who nonetheless fail to qualify for 'retirement' (public pension support)? A recent analysis of the working population, defined as aged 16-59/64, (Hutton, 1995) described a 30/30/40 society, with a disadvantaged 30 per cent, a 'newly insecure' 30 per cent, and an advantaged 40 per cent. Projecting such a cohort forward by thirty years might reveal a proportion of the currently advantaged in the privatised positions described above, able to make their own choices about a self-supported retirement through deferred earnings (pensions) savings and capital assets. The 'newly insecure' group would presumably have lost only the novelty rather than the insecurity of their position, and be relying on negotiating the socially and economically ambiguous stretch that is opening up between work-exit and publicly funded retirement, at which point in time they could either join the disadvantaged, in a category which ranges from marginalisation to exclusion; or if past employment has placed them just above the level of state retirement support, they would presumably carry on in self-supporting mode, the permanently insecure, until such time as depleted savings led to disadvantaged status. The insecure group would also be swelled by those of the previously advantaged group who had failed to defer or save enough income.

Although this scenario is employment/income centred, as Hutton observes, the role of inheritance and capital assets cannot currently be relied upon in the later-life security equation. The scale of the social policy issues before an ageing society are thus beginning to be appreciated. And although such considerations seem a distance away from educational needs for and about later life, the same question about an ageing society's view of its older members lies at the root of both. As Moody (1993) notes, it the notion of productive ageing that seems to have achieved dominance as the answer to the question "what is later life for?" He argues that older peoples' continued interest in economic participation will be taken seriously by policy makers who seek 1) a reduction in costs from 'surplus dependency', 2) an expansion of a marginal labour supply in anticipation of shortage, 3) a drive to displace human services out of the public and into the private sphere, reducing the need for tax increases (p 37).

So if ageing is to become productive, what price fulfilment? Shall it be a luxury, open to the advantaged who may, after all, have had it during their working lives as well, according to Laslett? Or perhaps, framed within the older adults' self-help and (self) advocacy movements, self-fulfilment becomes a rallying cry for the insecure and disadvantaged to challenge the social implications of their economic position, and create roles and 'productivity' of their own choosing. Moody pursues the question of values at this point also. He proposes that productive ageing holds an attraction for advanced societies in the late twentieth century because we honour and measure success through money, power, fame etc. This cultural 'ideal' presents us with a problem when powers (finally) diminish or fail, and makes the 'need to be needed' in late life a source of despair.

> We need instead a wider vision of what late-life productivity may mean, a vision that includes values such as altruism, citizenship, stewardship, creativity and the search for faith. We need to honour and cultivate these values. (p 38).

Holstein (1994) argues that modern culture is silently negative about later life, offering few resources for finding meaning and for knowing what kind of life is worth living. (p 21) The modern sense of self-respect, she suggests, values freedom, self-control, avoids suffering, and roots well-being in productive activity and family life. Some aspects of these characteristics could be problematic for older people, whose later life transitions need therefore to include the development of new sources of dignity and self-definition. Productive activity could remain as an option for those who wish it (conferring a sense of independence, respect, membership of a work community with rights and responsibilities etc.) as long as this is not seen as the only source of such senses, or constituting the most important dimension of later life. Indeed, the productive vision of later life cannot be the dominant paradigm for the following reasons, she suggests (p 21):

The non-economic aspects of life (eg. sense of community, non-material motivations for activity) have been missed in recent years, and because older people's contributions can be expressed in ways that are other than work-related, they may be all the more welcome. Second, there is a growing understanding that the larger sources of self identity and socially-relevant activity can be more available to older people who have time to access them, and these do not depend on the values that are relevant to mid-life. Third, the 'no-difference' stance of productive ageing, emphasising the positive features and continued capabilities of later life risks transferring ageism to the minority who do experience limitation, disability, or chronic illness. May not the minority pursue personal fulfilment and productivity without denying their dependency? Continuing to find meaning in situations where loss is a factor needs to remain an option for later life, but the ageing society which continues to value productivity so highly will find this a difficult response to make.

Creating the climate for the emergence of learning opportunities that help make these choices clearer will also be a difficulty until the ageing society through its policy makers and opinion leaders begins seriously to address these issues. Such are the challenges principally to policy makers but also to *employers and organisations and their agents, practitioners*. The challenges to these groups will be discussed in the remainder of this chapter. The actions of these may be influenced by the *theorists and researchers* who generate new ways of understanding, and also by *third and fourth agers and their advocates* who seek recognition and support for their agenda for change. The challeges of the ageing society to these second two groups will be discussed in Chapter 12, as public education and social advocacy.

As discussed earlier, the educational contribution to promoting agendas for later life are broadly in the areas of empowerment, participation, generational solidarity (interdependency) and the development of a sense of self in relation to society. How are these agendas being perceived and responded to by the first set of groups mentioned above?

The challenge to organisations and practitioners

Moody (1993) argues that for those who sponsor the development or support the provision of, or attendance at, education for older adults, or who are practitioners of it, the main obstacle has been a failure to regard it seriously enough. Older people's learning is only peripheral to the concern of all kinds of (post-school) educational establishments, as show by almost any indicator - numbers enroled, resources committed, sophistication of delivery systems etc. Despite its increasingly demonstrable links with continuing productivity, health and independence (for example), later life learning is not treated with importance because it produces neither grants for educational institutions nor career training paths for practitioners.

As a teaching/learning activity, however valuable, it remains almost entirely a consumer enterprise, Moody suggests. Even the most influential adult continuing education courses are essentially market-driven, responding to student or corporate demand, and earning fees according to what the market can bear. The contribution of such programmes to their host institutions is therefore different from traditional sources of academic prestige, especially in research-oriented universities. In the UK, university departments of continuing education might well identify with Moody's observations, as they struggle for status within their academic communities as well as for a modus operandi within new funding structures. Moody extends his argument to community colleges, many of which offer tuition-free access to older learners, but do not support older adult programmes as such. A parallel, if different, problem at British tertiary level (Colleges of Further Education, Adult Education Services) relates to major changes in funding and governance which has shifted the overwhelming balance of support to vocational programmes. A consequent move to accredit a wide variety of learning opportunities may have had the effect of restricting supply of, and access to, courses that had previously attracted older learners.

The heterogeneity of older students guarantees that some will indeed continue to value and pursue more vocationally oriented programmes. But many will miss the 'traditional' liberal education style offerings that are now difficult to make available except on a full-cost market basis. The higher fees now required make previously popular courses non-viable. Pre-retirement courses in the FE/Adult sectors have been demonstrated as suffering a loss of provision nationwide, (Gilbert, 1995) for example.

This vulnerability in the new market conditions calls for creative solutions. Moody suggests that the marginal status of programmes patronised by older learners has produced novel forms such as Elderhostel, which offers fixed prices and low marginal costs. This makes it popular with students and colleges and therefore successful, (200,000 participants per year). But the lack of overheads received, low levels of earnings retained and absence of public funding attached to what is, in effect, a voluntary movement means that educational institutions can only be interested in Elderhostel programmes as a consumer product. Income cannot be sufficient to also generate research and development.

Similar difficulties might also attach to other older adult targeted provision both in the USA and in Britain, where an embryonic 'senior studies' movement is emerging in Universities and Colleges. In Europe another 'novel form', the University of the Third Age, has retained (with varying degrees) an independence of educational institutions. Meanwhile, the mainstreaming trend in British higher education may prove a double-edged sword when applied to part-time programmes previously patronised by older students. At times of great pressure, due to legislative and funding change as well as to cuts in educational budgets at all levels, the voice for older adults' learning needs to be heard. First, the right message needs to be decided.

Our policy on older-adult education has take the wrong strategic turn. (It) operates at the margin not the center, and is constructed as a form of leisure-time activity, not human capital investment. . . (it) has developed almost entirely separate from the 'ageing enterprise' activities of human services (e.g. health and social welfare). Later-life learning is perceived by gerontologists as a frill for the well-to-do, not as a strategy for solving problems of the less-advantaged elderly. This strategic orientation towards individual learning outside of social structure has had devastating results for older adult education, depriving it of any wider legitimation. (Moody, 1993, p. 224).

In keeping with the times, then, should the leisure-oriented, consumerist conception of older adult education be allowed to wither, and be superseded by education (at all ages) that is more oriented towards production? In other words, does the concept of productive ageing offer a politically promising new strategy for the promotion of older adult's learning? Since elsewhere in the economy education is linked at some level to jobs, why not seek to conceptualise and organise older adult education to both paid and unpaid work in later life? By extension then, why not include in the argument for older adults' learning the retaining / training elements of publicly funded programmes that support employment for adults generally? This link has not been made except, as is often the case, for a few pioneering projects that have focused successfully on remotivating and re-skilling older unemployed people.

Recent research on the employment of older workers (variously defined, but usually 40+) has built a picture of difficulties and conflicting beliefs and practices in the areas of recruitment and selection processes, training and career advancement, retention and redundancy policies, early exit and retirement practices, employee guidance, counselling and other forms of personal support. Notions of good practice involving older employees are beginning to be networked informally and on a European level, producing what has been termed a movement for 'positive age-related human resources management'. This must surely be an area of concern and possible contribution for educators as well as gerontologists. The links that could thereby be forged to greater effect are the concepts of lifelong continuing education, training and educational guidance, and career and later life planning (which latter group now includes the proper concerns of pre-retirement education).

This broad educational context against which the learning needs of older people (whether currently employed or not) could be promoted has recently been acknowledged in a National Institute for Adult Continuing Education (NIACE) campaign. Entitled *Older and Bolder* the NIACE initiative set out (in 1995) to encourage educational institutions (higher, further and adult education services) to perceive and provide for older adults as learners. Their launch document for the campaign offers this view in support of their intentions:

> There is now widespread acknowledgment that a key factor in redressing the economic balance is to increase and enhance the productive skills base of the whole population; that job-specific training needs to be supported by broad, liberal educational programmes which allow for the development of flexible and communicative citizens; and also that continuing education can prolong healthy active life. However, analysing the problem and achieving the solution rarely come together through less-than well-oiled policy machinery so that the full range of lifelong learning opportunities are not yet available, far less being delivered for all. (NIACE, 1995).

Here we see the re-negotiated place for the 'broad liberal educational programmes' as supports for the productive skills base for all people at all ages. Flexibility and communication are particularly desirable outcomes, it is suggested. NIACE's chief targets for their campaign to promote older people's participation in education are the programme planners and practitioners. Hartford (1990) commented on the preparation needs of practitioners of all kinds who work with older people, but made special reference to adult educators. She considered that not only did the education or training involved in professional preparation need to affect the attitudes of practitioners, but it also required their becoming equipped with methodologies to help others examine and change their philosophies and values related to ageing and ageism.

These others included fellow practitioners and organisational decision makers, other individuals, and society at large. Most particularly practitioners would need to be prepared to help older adults avoid the self fulfilling stereotypes provided by an ageist society. Hartford suggests three strategies that future adult educators should consider. These were:- developing senior adult education programmes with curricula that value social relationships and a sense of adequacy as highly as any subject matter considerations; developing competencies that will assist preparation for new careers after 60; devising intellectually stimulating provision for those in residential homes or hospital who would otherwise be prevented from participating by physical disability.

Applying her argument to practitioners in all human service fields Hartford notes that practically all workers in these areas will spend part of their careers in practice with, or on behalf of, older adults. Moreover, an increasing proportion of workers will specialise in existing or new areas of work directly related to older adults. Initial professional and continuing education will be required for their preparation and professional development. Hartford surmises that the rate of social change will demand greater flexibility in its human service practitioners. Professional preparation will therefore need to include in-depth mastery of a range of social and human issues as well as technical skills in education, therapy, and the development of individuals and groups. At the administrative level, skills would be needed in planning and programme management, co-ordination and collaboration of services, community organisation and change. All these would be in addition to the attitudinal and values content indicated earlier.

In trying to envisage future 'student bodies' for professional education for the human services, Hartford predicts three main groups. First, young people seeking initial careers, wishing to 'vocationalise' their college education by adding an occupational element to a solid academic background. Such workers are often motivated by periods of work practice with (for e.g.) older people's services of various kinds, whereafter they feel a commitment to improving such services. Second, an interest in the practice of social gerontology is shown by people seeking second careers, usually with relevant experience to bring to human services. They seek a new career through disenchantment or redundancy in their first field, or as returners to the labour market from homemaking, often with a personal as well as a professional motive to improve society's response to human need. Third, older people themselves, having taken early retirement may increasingly become involved vocationally in human services (perhaps starting on a voluntary basis).

Hartford observes that, for the second and third groups especially, professional or career education would be best advised to build on what they know already, rearrange knowledge and values, offer new skills and a means to change attitudes. It will need to acknowledge the threat and anxiety that is often involved in mid or later life career change. She recommends that older and early retired people could be especially considered for such vocational roles in society.

> We need to be more innovative in developing career education opportunities to prepare older adults to become human service workers - gerontologists themselves - who design programs, develop services, administer organizations, and teach courses for their peers, not only on a volunteer basis but on a regular professional level. (Hartford, 1990, p. 193).

The growing phenomenon of leadership by older adults in the voluntary sector is cited as evidence for their professional potential. Lastly, Hartford warns that some responsibility for placement in jobs following training should be accepted by educators, institutions and, indeed, the ageing society that needs their skills and experience.

The case of leadership training for retirement education

All of the above analysis and comment, concerning the need for education and training opportunities that prepare people for teaching and managing human services for older adults, and concerning relevant curricula and potential students, applies particularly well to the case of (pre-) retirement education. There does indeed need to be a conceptual and practical understanding on the part of the would-be practitioner of the range of human and social issues involved in retirement. Existing knowledge and values will require reappraisal, attitudes and their role in practice will need to be challenged. Repertoires of skills will not only require extension, but also to be acquired in such a way that practitioners will be able to update them and communicate them to others.

Brahce and Hunter (1990) note that the increasing body of knowledge about retirement itself has implications for (pre) retirees and, correspondingly, for the training of professionals to be engaged in planning and carrying out educational programmes. They make four observations about such training in relation to the contemporary and future nature of retirement:- the need to keep up-to-date in our understanding of how people adjust to the mid and later life stages of ageing; the wholesale questioning of the concept of retirement, and its relationship to policies and practices that tend to promote either dependency or activity; the need to constantly review assumptions about work and retirement, as many differences relate to gender, occupational level and age cohort (rather than age per se); the recognition that retirement is a continuing, complicated process, which impacts on individuals and families in differing ways, and in differing degrees.

So although retirement education has traditionally helped individuals and their spouses understand and adjust to retirement-related change, Brahce and Hunter further suggest that

> Gerontologists need not only be concerned with preparation for retirement, but even more urgently, to determine the educational needs of men and women throughout the later years, and following retirement. (p. 272)

This call to root training for pre-retirement within a wider professional concern for older adults' education in general may seem surprising to readers outside the USA where, it is understood, gerontology has become available (as part or as a whole) of courses in both initial and continuing professional education. Brahce and Hunter, however, observe that, in the higher education sector, the emphasis within gerontology education is on graduate instruction or career training, rather than on the professional preparation of those who are in a position to develop pre and post-retirement education programmes. But they also acknowledge the role of other agencies involved in educational programming and services for older people, with whom Universities and colleges should keep in touch if they wish to enter this area of training. Furthermore, educational institutions should be ready to respond when community or civic groups call upon them for gerontological knowledge and understanding whether for the purposes of trainer training, or older adult education itself.

Indeed the key to developing the quantity and quality of pre-retirement programmes must surely be the preparation of leaders who can offer quality-assured educational services to middle-aged and older people. Accredited courses, at post-graduate level, in pre-retirement education principles and practice are offered at some American Universities, most usually those with gerontology centres. With relatively few UK universities having gerontological studies, let alone centres, there is one known accredited course specifically in pre-retirement education and planning, and possibly one or two further gerontology-related courses that are followed by would-be pre-retirement educators. Short courses on aspects of pre-retirement education content or methodology are occasionally held by a range of organisations and agencies, or their related professional associations, which have interests in pre-retirement education.

As in the field of gerontology generally, American literature on the principles and practice of pre-retirement education is greater in volume than are British or European writings on these matters. There has been more research on the impact of retirement generally, and on particular groups within the older population. There are more publications that seek to advise pre-retirement educators by linking theory and practice (see for example Riker and Myers, 1990; Hayes and Deren, 1990 and Richardson, 1993) Interestingly, the conclusions they draw and the futures they predict translate fairly well to the European scene, given that the common factor of Western industrialised society relates so closely to the nature and experience of retirement.

To summarise the above American authors' views will hopefully be helpful to pre-retirement education wider afield, by comparison and application to other settings. The major training requirement is seen as the ability to translate real, life-directed needs into educational programmes. The nature of these programmes (the end product towards which training is directed) they suggest contains such elements as:- Giving older people understanding of the changes in which they and others are involved; the imparting of knowledge and skills relevant to later life / retirement living; the offering of a real opportunity to build on interests, abilities and personal resources generally towards a plan or purpose for later life; and lastly, providing a positive learning experience.

In order to orchestrate programmes that demonstrate some or all of these characteristics, pre-retirement educators' training will require a frame of reference that locates the mid and later life stages of ageing, and the nature of the retirement process. This theoretical understanding will need to be matched by an experience in planning, conducting and evaluating programmes designed for retirement transition. Lastly, the skills of effective promotion, coordination of resources and gaining of sponsorship for programmes would then enable the professional to function.

It ought to be noted that Europe is not entirely bereft of pre-retirement training literature, though small in amount. This also reflects the outline for training described above and encourages and guides practitioners on matters such as working with adult groups, negotiating pre-retirement course agendas with participants as well as sponsors, understanding contemporary retirement and ageing issues (UK examples; Coleman and Chiva, 1991 and Walker, 1992).

In predicting issues for training and practice of pre-retirement education in the future, and in relation to an ageing society here are some of the factors highlighted, again mainly by American commentators:

- Future cohorts of retirees will have higher levels of general educational attainment, and may (i) respond to opportunities for lifelong education differently, (ii) require pre-retirement education that takes this into account.
- The trend to early retirement may be softened to a more phased or gradual withdrawal from the workforce, with intermittent periods of full or part-time re-entry, retraining, volunteering, caring etc.
- The greater participation of women in employment will increase their experience of retirement, and preparation will need to reflect more accurately women's concerns and experience.
- The eventual acceptance of the idea of a learning society, with lifelong education and training, will alter the educational context of mid-life and pre-retirement preparation.
- Related to this, providing for the greater demand for vocational training in mid and later life may be seen as a corporate responsibility by employers and unions, along with pension and other employee benefits.
- Educational institutions may give greater credence to life-centred education and training, leading to more multi-disciplinary programmes and the introduction of gerontological content within a greater range of specialised professional fields.
- It is likely that the numbers experiencing retirement will grow, and the forms that retirement will take will increase, leading to new retirement issues for pre-retirement educators to identify. It is predicted that the most relevant ones will be poverty, involuntary retirement, and marital and family pressures.
- Increased understanding of socio-economic factors will be needed if

programmes are to address the concerns of disadvantaged groups such as women and ethnic minorities, whose worklife inequalities will transmit into retirement.

- The dimensions of family structures, caregiving and long-term marriage are under-researched for their effects on retirement, yet pre-retirement education requires a current understanding and approach to contemporary pressures.

We need retirement counsellors who know about retirement, retirement inequalities and problems; who are well trained and sensitive to (older people's) diverse experience. Retirement counsellors who use a psychosocial approach, examining individual and systemic problems concurrently, will emphasize emancipation of the client from oppressive forces. . . . . Retirement counsellors must be flexible and open-minded and work on many levels. . . . Multiple intervention strategies are frequently employed. In all cases the goal is the same: to alleviate suffering and create more satisfactory retirement experiences for older persons, . . . and help people of all backgrounds. (Richardson, 1993, p. 206-7).

12 Public education and social advocacy

Joanna Walker

The challenge to research and theory

Much of the American literature referred to in the preceding chapter recognises that, despite the developments in the field of gerontology, the bulk of pre-retirement education practice has changed its understanding of retirement very little since the 1960s and 70s. Its unexamined assumption is still of a leisure-oriented, financial security framework, with little concern for fulfilment of broader developmental issues. Yet older people express a desire for a greater experience of learning, and opportunities to 'do something for society'.

However, the third age model of retirement has certainly encouraged the view of later life as a period of personal growth and societal enhancement through contribution, creativity and caring (Migliaccio and Corbett, 1993). Add to this the even more recent emphasis on productivity to achieve economic security as well as for social solidarity, and a picture of retirement in an ageing society begins to emerge that is more in tune with the times.

In the hope that future pre-retirement educators will be in greater contact with adult educators, whose concern will increasingly be with lifelong continuing education, what further help can gerontologists offer practitioners in order to increase understanding of later life and its educational needs? Weiland (1995) recommends that we re-visit the historical construction of ageing itself to see how it has shaped the self-concepts and educational interests of older learners themselves, and also the projects and goals of gerontologists.

As an example of placing newly emerging understandings of later life within an historical framework, he cites the 'natural history of the life course' which has moved from a religious to a secular and scientific mode. The old Protestant version of life as a voyage - which encouraged introspection, self-motivation, receiving as well as creating wisdom and understanding, continually reconciling past and

131

future in the present, and giving oneself up to a higher power - constituted a highly workable model for generating both continuity and meaning.

The present day version of the life course offers rational, even predictable, stages and opportunities for intervention and control. Modern morality organises itself around the virtues of independence, health and worldly success, sowing the seeds Weiland argues for the modern form of ageism. That is, the splitting apart of positive and negative aspects of growing older, and the ideology that with sufficient (modern) virtue, ageing individuals can achieve the positive and avoid the negative. This dualistic view of ageing would have been a false dichotomy in pre-scientific thinking, up until the Victorians developed modern ambitions for *mastery* to replace the older acceptance of *mystery*.

This historical analysis is not repeated in order to glorify a lost era of understanding, merely to illustrate that the same epistemological problems exist in gerontological theory and research today. Within the philosophical and methodological framework of interpretive social science, where most social gerontologists work, there are both *existential* questions about meaning (in order to make sense of one's experience) and *scientific* questions about meaning which seek to develop logical, reliable, interpretable and predictive theories.

Recognising the role of both these enterprises in the production of knowledge may help. It locates the problem which many gerontologists feel but cannot identify clearly concerning, for example, the conflict between what a person knows from a lifetime of experience and what (s)he cannot and does not know about ageing. This parallels the theoretical difficulty mentioned above, that we are stalled in a dualistic view of ageing, which double-mindedness makes it difficult to combat society's continuing discrimination and ageism, because our attempts to assert older people's capacity for growth and productivity are perceived as lacking in conviction.

Other commentators have noted the implications of this position; Moody talks of the 'colonisation of welfare' in later life and ageing, referring to the entrepreneurial activities of welfare services and professionals creating new spheres of responsibility for themselves by entering at those points of intervention offered by the modern bureaucratised life-course. In 1993, Moody berated not only educators for not taking older adult education seriously enough, but also gerontologists whose intellectual field is still dominated by the 'failure model' of ageing, he claims (p. 222).

This is because the external interests that have supported the growth of gerontology have largely been those health and social welfare services that provide not only the job market for gerontologists, but also encourage the research and training funds from government and other agencies. So despite the fact that the subject matter of gerontology is the whole span of later life experience, the dominant professional interests cast older people as clients, patients and occasionally consumers, but not often as learners.

Can the dualist view of ageing, and its alleged continuing preference for the negative, be sufficiently overcome? Can the ageing society move beyond this to re-interpret the more holistic, and some would say realistic, view of later life which accepts 'the ambiguity, contingency, intractability and unmanageability of human life'? (Weiland, 1995 p. 603)

Towards the end of his analysis of models of ageing in recent and current research (discussed in Chapter one of this text) Marshall (1993) debates the relative contribution of quantitative and qualitative methods of investigation, and their engagement with data in a meaningful way. The point he makes is that there is no substitute for good conceptualisation whatever methodology or techniques are employed. If gerontology's concern is to offer enriched and creative understanding of ageing and later life, then qualitatively expressed concepts, which he calls metaphors, can be valuable and may capture a more holistic picture. He offers three such metaphors that he feels have potential for future research and theorising:

First, the metaphor of an ageing individual moving across time and through the life course can be described as travelling in a *convoy of social relations* rather than in 'solo passage'. A ship travelling in company with others is a helpful image through which to interpret the changes during the journey in leadership, in support, in communication, resourcing, or disability and drop-out from the convoy. Marshall locates the concept underlying this metaphor as that of ageing as intersecting trajectories.

Second, the familiar metaphor of the cohort, setting off from the same place together and marching through time, is given the added dimension of a fan, with narrow base and progressively broader span. This signifies the ageing process as an *increasingly differentiated cohort*, calling for explanation of the mechanisms that tend to make people less alike over a period of time.

Third, the metaphor of life as the story rather than the journey, with the ageing individual as author or editor, revising material for the *last chapter*. The actions and purposes associated with late life are therefore seen as the task of making sense of the past and present, and accepting the finality of the future. This metaphor relates to several developmental concepts such as life review processes, and Erikson's eighth stage.

Marshall makes no apology for the fairly concrete nature of these 'metaphors' which are intended to inspire imaginative conceptualisation of later life, leading to testable propositions and, thus, scientific understanding. Concluding on the future contributions of gerontology, Marshall notes the current hegemony of the life-course perspective (although his metaphors seem to have echoes of the outmoded paradigm of ageing as 'life's journey'). Where the dualist conflict (positive vs. negative ageing) produces an emphasis on 'medicalised ageing', stressing the negative or needy aspects requiring social intervention, this is because gerontologists have failed to contextualise the study of ageing as a life long process as opposed to the situation of being old(er).

It could be suggested that life transitions are as much a growth industry perhaps for psychologists and therapists, in the same way as it has been for social workers operating on the deficit model. However, the leading edge for life course research could be to differentiate between the relatively 'scheduled' life-transitions and normative events that can be expected if not timed, (e.g. death, parenthood, retirement) and non-normative but common events that cannot be scheduled (e.g. illness, divorce). In this way a life course picture of relatively durable strains in daily life, scheduled or transitional events, plus less expected events, could be built up.

Given that life course perspectives in gerontology seek to integrate individual and group characteristics into a framework of historical time and social structure, how well does this approach reflect 'real people with real histories'? This is the question Blaikie (1992) asked, suggesting that gerontologists had indeed failed 'to imagine and embellish concepts that incorporate the fluidity of personal and social change over time'. (p. 2)

He laments the insufficient research attention paid to age as a variable in the same way that class, race and gender have been, to great effect on our understanding of how these permeate the whole of life. In taking for granted the pervasiveness of ageing (i.e. age at any life stage) it has not been recognised as an organising principle or social structure. Although adulthood is the longest phase of the life course, it is the least researched. Perhaps because of the lack of imperative from the welfare colonists who have been more concerned with the problems of youth and much older age, adult life for the majority has been perceived as relatively problem free, at least in terms of public spending needs.

Now of course, as Blaikie and many others point out, the chronological bonds by which one could predict schooling, initial training, marriage, parenthood, work exit / retirement, disability and death are now highly variable. Significant changes in the labour market and family formation and dissolution provide further uncertainties. 'If the earlier twentieth century witnessed the emergence and consolidation of retirement as a fixed phase, then its closing decade reveals a growing fragmentation' (Blaikie, 1993, p. 3).

The older population has never (in recent times) been more divided: retirement for many involves economic dependency and the possibility of dwindling quality of life; but for some it is third age fulfilment, retirement 'lifestyle' and continuing prosperity. There is also a health divide epitomised by the crossing from the third to the fourth age, but also reflected in the differential health effects of available services, environment, and relative poverty. There is a growing cultural divide, it is suggested, between the active productive older person and those who seek leisure, or who are ill or disabled.

The gerontologist who seeks to make sense of such diversity at a social as well as a personal level, and thus be of service to adult educators, would do well to pursue their study within a *life course development framework*, Blaikie suggests. This has the advantages of including personal biographical awareness, enabling reflection and planning; it also addresses psychological concerns about predictable crises and transition and their resolution, often related to socially mediated life events, such as normative or age / stage related influences ('generational' effects). The picture of ageing thus produced is not only socially constructed but, because of the incorporation of notions of personal change, also descriptive of 'the making of individuals in each epoch'.

Blaikie's lifecourse approach is in the gerontological tradition of gathering ideas from various social and behavourial sciences and re-grouping them into an interdisciplinary design. His declared intention is to emphasise the longer term of adult life as a whole, through the exploration of the points where individuals and societies meet. As testament to the educational relevance of his approach, the Masters programme in Life Course Development which Blaikie pioneered at London University during the 1980s is followed by mature students of various professional backgrounds, some with the intention of developing their roles as older adult educators.

The challenge to older people and their advocates - agendas for educational gerontology

Morris (1993) in a concluding and future-oriented chapter of an edited text on ageing identifies his primary concern as *defining the place of older people in twenty-first century society*. The two major social issues of enhancing the life of the individual and building the strength of the collectivity can be contextualised for older people by asking (i) does society need the contributions of all its citizens, at all ages, and (ii) does a satisfying ageing require socially meaningful roles as well as material security?

If the answer to either or both of these is yes, there is a role for educational gerontology. Morris suggests that the twentieth century has not yet resolved whether or how to use society's resources in order both to seek personal gratification and to create social systems acceptable to multiple group interests. The implication is that unless older people take action as a class or in related movements, they will never gain the resources from which to shape services, products and further access to decision making.

As part of our provision for 'the losers in life's competition' collective obligation for older people is seen as being satisfied by a mature system of social security, a partial private pension system, and the freedom of obligation to seek paid work. Retirees' continued occupation of life space for a further twenty, thirty, forty years even is primarily a personal matter. This virtual absence of discussion of the collective responsibility and involvement in the ageing process illustrates a deep age-bias in many institutions of modern life. Despite the wishes of older adults, with lifetimes of experience to offer, their social disengagement is still the prevailing wish of the rest of society, Morris proposes (p. 289). However this attitude is unsatisfactory, and may not be sustainable for several reasons. These could be the pressure points for older adults and their advocates:

Even those who are in a position (materially) to 'do nothing', up to a half wish to be involved in something other than self-gratification; employing institutions (economic and voluntary) will eventually find it difficult to maintain their activities efficiently with fewer young workers, and without the mature talents of older people; there is increasing evidence of disaffection with the choices currently open to the 'retired', with insufficient jobs for those who want them, unsatisfying recreation and scattered or distant families.

Rather than attempting simply to increase the choices available in order for retirees to realise their private aspirations, Morris emphasises the citizenship role of older adults. That is to say, the rights of individuals to work, non-work, retirement etc. are dependent on general levels of responsibility that everyone takes to maintain a society that makes these rights possible. Whilst personal freedom has on the whole increased it has not been accompanied by collective interdependency. There is less paid work, volunteering, community involvement, or political and civic involvement. We are generally speaking more individualised, with older people further out on the margins. The ageing society requires a pro-active movement for involvement, for recognition and valuing contributions at all ages.

Morris' suggestions for public education and advocacy are:

1. Clarifying that new technology is a mechanism for using older adults' skills, not a bar to their use (both in terms of production, and training and communication).
2. Promoting the labour-force and volunteer work potential of older people.
3. Broadening the base of volunteer activity, and better dissemination of opportunities, requirements, etc.

4. Developing indicators of value for non-paid work, to enhance its social recognition.
5. Producing a set of 'explicit niches' in society for which older adult talents could be specifically engaged.
6. Improving the means for midlife and pre-retired people to express views about how they would employ their next twenty years.

Other agendas for action have been generated by educational gerontologists. Schuller and Walker (1990) proposed an 'educational agenda for the third age' organised around these principles:-

1. Full recognition of older people as learners and teachers, including measures to reduce ageism that inhibits such recognition.
2. Provision of a wide range of learning opportunities, and reducing the unhelpful vocational/non-vocational divide.
3. Recognition of the role of educational guidance and counselling for older adults.
4. Encouragement for far greater collaboration between educational providers, informal and formal, education and non-education sectors.
5. Improvement in training for workers in this field, perhaps on an inter-agency basis.
6. The provision of material support to older students, and to institutions to encourage both demand and supply (Schuller and Walker, 1990, p. 22).

In 1982 Groombridge set out a case addressed to society at large, to promote the importance of later life education.

1. Education fosters self-reliance and independence from the need of extra social resources.
2. Education enables older people to cope with numerous practical and personal challenges in a complex, changing world.
3. Education for and by older people strengthens their actual or potential contribution to society.
4. The ability to communicate awareness and interpretation of experience to other generations is a valuable role that preserves and develops perspective and understanding within a changing society.
5. Education is vital as a means for expression and learning.

A campaign to promote these kinds of principles was launched in the UK in 1981, entitled the Forum for Rights of Elderly to Education (FREE). It operated for ten years or so, producing a newsletter and disseminating information on relevant activities and developments from across many sectors and disciplines. Its information role has recently been incorporated within Age Concern England's Policy and Information Department.

The pensioner movement itself, in the UK at least, has sought greater collaboration and co-ordination between its constituent organisations, as expressed by the formation of an umbrella Pensioners' Convention in the early 1990's.The Convention had been meeting as an informal coalition of various older people's organisations during the 1980s. Relaunched around 1990 in order to provide a better focus for communicating older people's interests, the Pensioners Convention continues to formalise its structure and ways of working, and to hold regular national meetings. An all party Parliamentary lobby group on pensioners issues has been officially recognised and housed at Westminster since the mid 1970s, with paid staff. The formation of Pensioners Forums was investigated in the early 1990s with a view to disseminating a modus operandi for potential groups (PRA, 1992). The Pensioners' Parliament at European level has attracted much interest, both from older Europeans and their societies at large. Formed to meet initially in Luxembourg it has met twice, in 1993 and 1994. Originally an initiative of the socialist group of MEPs, the Pensioners' Parliament's second meeting chose representatives on an all-party basis, reflecting the political make-up of the European Parliament. A third development has been to encourage national groupings or 'Parliaments' to meet, and a UK session was held in Blackpool in the summer of 1995.

All of the above developments, and others in the private (e.g. publishing) sphere are perhaps reflecting the dissatisfaction with current choices outlined by Morris. There is not space or opportunity to do justice to their significance here, but the evidence is mixed as to whether older people are increasingly making common cause where it is seen as appropriate or possible. The role of advocacy organisations is another important area of consideration, recognising the conflicting issues of who holds power and why, how change is effected, and according to whose agenda.

Whilst older people's organisations and advocacy groups campaign on a broad front, covering many issues that relate to educational matters in a contextual or tangential way, non (except the moribund 'FREE') campaigns directly or on a long-term basis for the expansion of later life learning opportunities or better training for human service workers from an older consumer's point of view. There may of course be local campaigns to save services, educational or health or welfare-related, or protests about particular items of political or legislative activity. For example, in Britain a budget proposal for Value Added Tax on domestic fuel, and legislative proposals to remove adult liberal education from within local authorities' realm of duty to provide, were two issues on which an 'older' voice was organised, heard and acted upon.

Moody (1987) emphasised that the ageing society needed to be so organised as to provide people with the resources necessary to pursue the things that make life worth living. Later life learning has been proposed throughout this text as a vehicle for meeting multiple needs, not least the hope that there is value in the later stages of life. Many in the educational gerontology field are indicating that it is time to move beyond the issue of access to educational opportunity, even if this has not been entirely resolved. Access may need to be redefined as allowing older people to take charge of their own development, acknowledging that disadvantage and marginalisation are present in relation to learning at all ages, and need not be conflated with older age as a problem.

Critical gerontologists would hold a differing view no doubt, citing gerontology's failure to engage with people's real needs, and its maintenance of a false neutrality on social issues. The past deficiency of social gerontology to acknowledge (for example) the social construction of the marginalisation of women or black people, or the structured dependency embedded in much social care and its related training, have their parallels in educational gerontology, it is suggested (Glendenning, 1995). We therefore need to ask such questions as whose interests are being served by older adults' education, and where the power lies in whatever educational process we are proposing. At least part of the role of education should lead to self fulfilment *via* an understanding on the part of older people about where they are located in the social structure and the factors that have shaped that location.

Peterson (1990) who has been so influential in the short history of educational gerontology identifies these issues for its future:-

- The challenge to deal with the issues of ageing and ageism *within* programmes designed for older people, whatever their subject content.
- A challenge to educational institutions and educational authorities to identify funding for older adult's programming.
- Improvement in the quality and efficacy of educational provision, via evaluation, better training for course leadership, more informed guidance from advisory or governing bodies etc.
- An expanded but intelligent use of mass media and high technology resources for learning.
- Encouragement to the corporate sector to invest in continuing education and training for adults especially from mid-life onwards.
- The challenge to attract marginalised or disadvantaged elders to programmes, taking account of lower educational backgrounds, literacy or coping skills deficits, language or ethnic barriers.

- Acknowledging that elder education is interventionist by nature, what outcomes should we seek to bring about as a priority? (suggestions include literacy, problem solving, prevention of possible problems, contributive or productive skills, influential and empowerment skills, role development for employment or volunteering, and self-actualisation).

Peterson concludes that since all items of this last list are worthy of pursuit for older people, growth may well occur in them all but, since resources are so scarce, predominance will be shown by those programmes that attract the most participants for the least outlay - that is those that are recreational and social. He urges educational gerontologist to exert what influence they have to also gain support for other kinds of courses which have outreach and outcomes of social value as features.

Peterson's conclusion begs the question as to whether educational gerontology should aspire to being interventionist, and whether it could succeed even if this were agreed, taking us back to some of the arguments rehearsed in Chapter four. Thorson and Waskel (1990) observe that although in the 1970s it was common for educationists to call for instrumental skills teaching for the elderly, it is now clear that such survival skills as are truly needed are learned independently by older people over the life course, and in meeting life's challenges.

They go on to argue that there is, in fact, very little case for any different kind of adult education for most older people, compared with adults generally. This is because the third age brings little qualitative difference in educational needs compared with middle age, since even joblessness is a common experience. Although Laslett may not agree, the educational approach would be essentially the same for a 49 year old as for a 70 year old, they suggest. It is, rather, the much older person who may need educational gerontology *as an intervention* in the sense that it makes a unique difference to their situation. Also there would be a qualitative difference in (for example) teaching self-maintenance to a dementia sufferer, or life review to a dying person, or enabling a recently widowed person to achieve social re-engagement. In the future there will be many more much older people, and they may be more alone in society.

Education for the third age is happening and will continue, they argue, due to consumer demand and the recognition of new markets for educational services. Educators and other human service practitioners will increasingly be called upon to work in an educational mode with older, frailer people. Meanwhile older people in general will be freely mixing work, leisure, education and personal growth, without regard for age in ways we find it hard to imagine today (Birren, 1987).

On a final note, the enduring quality of education for older people, as well as younger ones, is the opportunity it provides for both learning and socialisation.

Commentators who enthuse about the information superhighway and information technology in general sometimes fail to recognise the irreplaceable elements of learning in the company of others.

Innovative technologies can sustain life, provide independence and improve rehabilitation and, of course, calculate and communicate at great speed, so increasing available information. Whilst resource-based and self-directed learning have a valuable and appropriate place in the range of learning methodologies, most people will also seek from an educational programme a framework of reasoning or meaning for their chosen subject, the motivation and means to study it and the skills to pursue it. Drawing a parallel with the activity of shopping, Thorson and Waskel observe

> People want to get out there and squeeze the melons; the act of shopping has intrinsic benefits that go beyond the acquisition of goods. We suspect that the same is true of education. (p. 344)

Bibliography

Allat, P. report of a workshop, 'Women into Retirement', January 1990 Pre-Retirement Association (unpublished) and cited in Walker, J. (1992)

Antonovsky, A. (1979), *Health, Stress and Coping: new perspectives on mental and physical well-being*, Jossey-Bass, San Francisco.

Arber, S. and Ginn, J. (1991), *Gender and Later Life: a sociological analysis of resources and constraints*, Sage Publications, London.

Baldwin, J. D. (1986), *George Herbert Mead: A Unifying Theory for Sociology*, Sage Publications, London.

Bass, S.A., Caro, F.G. and Chen, Y-P. (1993) *Achieving a Productive Aging Society*, Greenwood Publishing Group, Westport, Connecticut.

Battersby, D. (1990), 'From Androgogy to Gerogogy', Glendenning, F. and Percy, K. (eds.), *Ageing, Education and Society, readings in educational gerontology*, pp. 131-7, The Association for Educational Gerontology, Keele.

Battersby, D. (1992) 'A new Framework for Older Learners and its Implications for Pre-Retirement Education', speech delivered to Annual Meeting of Pre-Retirement Association, London.

Battersby, D. and Glendenning, F. (in prep), *Teaching and Learning in Later Life: a critical perspective on educational gerontology*, Arena Books, Aldershot.

Bauman, Z. (1992), *Mortality, Immortality and Other Life Strategies*, Polity Press, Cambridge.

Beck, E, (1992), *Risk Society*, Sage Publications, London.

Berne, E. (1964), *Games People Play*, Grove Press, New York.

Biggs, S. (1993), *Understanding Ageing*, Open University Press, Milton Keynes.

Birren, J. E. (1987), cited in *Aging Research on the Threshold of Discovery*, The Alliance for Aging Research, Washington, DC., p. 26.

Blaikie, A. (1992), 'Whither the Third Age? Implications for Gerontology', *Generations Review*, Vol. 12, No. 1, pp. 2-4.

Blakemore, K. and Boneham, M. (1994), *Age, Race and Ethnicity - a comparative approach*, Open University Press, Milton Keynes.

Bolton, C. (1990), 'Instructing Experienced Adult Learners', Sherron, R. and Lumsden, D.B. (eds.), *Introduction to Educational Gerontology* (3rd edition), pp 135-149, Hemisphere Publishing Corporation, New York.

Bone, M., Gregory, J., Gill, B. and Lader, B. (1992), *Retirement and Retirement Plans*, OPCS, HMSO, London.

Boswell, J. (1968), *Life of Johnson*, Vol. 1 1770, Folio Society of London. London.

Bowlby, J. (1979), *The Making and Breaking of Affectional Bonds*, Tavistock, London.

Bowlby, J. (1980), *Attachment and Loss*, Volume 3: *Loss*, Hogarth Press, London.

Brahce, C.I. and Hunter, N. N. (1990), 'Leadership Training for Retirement', in Sherron, R. and Lumsden, D.B. (eds.) *Introduction to Educational Gerontology* (3rd edition), pp. 269-95, Hemisphere Publishing Corporation, New York.

Bramwell, R. D. (1992), 'Beyond Survival: curriculum models for senior adult education', *Educational Gerontology*, Vol. 18, pp. 433-46.

Brusselmans, C. (1980), *Towards Moral and Religious Maturity*, International Conference on Moral and Religious Development, 1st Abbey of Senanque 1979, Silver Burdett Co, New Jersey.

Bury, M. (1982), 'Chronic Illness as Biographical Disruption', *Sociology of Health and Ilness*, Vol. 4, No. 2, pp 167-182.

Butler, R. N. and Gleason, H. P. (eds.) (1985), *Productive Aging, Enhancing Vitality in Later Life*, Springer Publishing Co. Inc., New York.

Carter, A. and Nash, C. (1992), *Pensioners Forums: a way to succeed - ideas on how to set up and run a Pensioners' Forum*, Pre-Retirement Association, Guildford.

Carter, A. and Nash, C. (1992), *Pensioners Forums: an active voice*, Pre-Retirement Association, Guildford.

Chappell, N. L. and Orbach, H. L. (1986), 'Socialization in Old Age: a Meadian Perspective', Marshall, V.W. (ed.), *Later Life: the Social Psychology of Ageing*, Sage Publications, London and Beverley Hills, pp. 75-106.

Chené, A. and Fleury, J-J. (1992), 'College Studies after 50 years of age', *Educational Gerontology*, Vol. 18, No. 5, pp. 497-510.

Chennek, S. (ed.) 1995), *Training Opportunities for Older Adults*, Open University Press, Milton Keynes.

Chiva, A. (1995), *Making the Most of Your Future: Retirement workbook*, Pre-Retirement Association, Guildford.

Cole, T. R. (1992), *The Journey of Life: a Cultural History of Ageing in America*, Cambridge University Press, Cambridge.

Coleman, A. (1983), *Preparation for Retirement in England and Wales*, National Institute of Adult Education, Leicester.

Coleman, A. and Chiva, A. (1991), *Coping with Change: focus on retirement*, Health Education Authority, London.

Cooper, M. and Bornat, J. (1988), 'Equal opportunity of special need: combatting the woolly bunny', *Journal of Educational Gerontology*, Vol. 3, No. 1, pp. 28-41.

Coppard, L. (1981), 'Lifelong Learning and the Elderly', Himmelstrup, P. et al (eds.), *Strategies for Lifelong Learning*, pp. 94-117, University Centre of South Jutland, Denmark, and the Association for Recurrent Education, United Kingdom.

Corbett, C. and Urquhart, N. (1990), *Comfort Zones, Leaders Guide* (2nd edit.), Crisp Publications, Inc., Los Altos, CA.

Cox, T. (1978), *Stress*, Macmillan Press, London.

Cumming, E. and Henry, W. (1961), *Growing Old: the process of disengagement*, Basic Books, New York.

Cunningham, W.R. and Brookbank, J.W. (1988), *Gerontology: The Psychology, Biology and Sociology of Aging*, Harper and Row, New York.

Dunn, H. L. (1973), *High Level Wellness*, Beatty, Arlington VA.

Eden, D., and Jacobsen, D. (1976), 'Propensity to retire among older executives', *Journal of Vocational Behaviour*, Vol. 8.

Elliot, J. (1993), *A General Theory of Bureaucracy*, Gregg revivals, Godstone.

Erickson, E.H. (1950, reprinted 1963), *Childhood and society*, Norton New York.

Featherstone, M. and Hepworth, M. (1989), 'Ageing and Old Age: Reflections on the Postmodern Life Course', Bytheway, B., Keil, T., Allatt, P. and Bryman, A. (eds.) *Becoming and Being Old: Sociological Approaches to Later Life*, pp.143-57. Sage Publications, London.

Festinger, L. (1957), *A Theory of Cognitive Dissonance*, RUW Peterson, Evanston, Illinois.

Fletcher, P. (1972), *Emotional Problems*, Pan Books Ltd., London.

Fromm, E. (1984), *The Fear of Freedom*, ARK Paperbacks, London. (original edition 1942.

Gadow, S. (1986), 'Frailty and Strength: the Dialectic of Ageing', Cole, T.R. and Gadow, S.A. (eds.), *What Does it Mean to Grow Old?: Reflections from the Humanities*, pp. 235-43, Duke University Press, Durham.

George, L.K. (1980), *Role Transitions in Later Life*, Wadsworth, Inc., Belmont, California.

George, L. K. (1990), 'Social Structure, Social processes and Social-psychological States', Binstock, R. H. and George, L. K. (eds.), *Handbook of Aging and the Social Sciences* (3rd edition), pp. 186-204, Academic Press, San Diego.

Giddens, A. (1990), *The Consequences of Modernity*, Polity Press, Cambridge.

Gilbert, H. (1995), 'Further Research into Provision of Courses in the Public Sector', Walker, J. (ed.), *PRA Yearbook and Directory of Mid-life retirement planning courses 1995/6*, pp. 2-5, Pre-Retirement Association, Guildford.

Ginsberg, L.H. and Datan, N. (1975), *Life-Span Developmental Psychology: normative life crises*, Academic Press, New York.

Glanz, D. and Neikrug, (1994), 'Making Aging Meaningful', *Ageing International*, June, pp. 23-6.

Glendenning, F. (ed.)(1985), *Educational Gerontology:International Perspectives*, Croom Helm, London.

Glendenning, F. (1989), 'Educational Gerontology in Britain as an Emerging Field of Study and Practice', *Educational Gerontology*, Vol. 15, No. 2, pp. 121-131.

Glendenning, F. (1990), 'The emergence of Educational Gerontology', Glendenning, F. and Percy, K. (eds.), *Education, Ageing and Society*, pp. 13-23, Association for Educational Gerontology, Keele, Staffs.

Glendenning, F. (1993), Letters to the editor, *Educational Gerontology*, Vol. 19, No. 1, pp. 87-8.

Glendenning, F. and Battersby, D. (1994), 'Foreword', Withnall, A. and Percy, K., *Good Practice in the Education and Training of Older Adults*, Arena, Aldershot.

Glendenning, F. and Percy, K. (eds.) (1990), *Education, Ageing and Society*, Association for Educational Gerontology, Keele, Staffordshire.

Glendenning, F. (1995), *The Development of Educational Gerontology and Gerontological Education*, paper given at British Society of Gerontology annual conference, University of Keele, 15 September.

Glendenning, F. and Stuart-Hamilton, I. (eds.) (1995), *Learning and Cognition in Later Life*, Arena Books, Aldershot.

Green, H. (1985), 'Informal Carers', *General Household Survey Supplement*, HMSO, London.

Groombridge, B. (1982),' Learning, Education and Later Life', *Adult Education*, Vol. 54, No. 4, pp. 314-25.

Handy, C. (1994), *The Empty Raincoat*, Hutchinson, London.

Harris, A. and Harris, T. (1985), *Staying OK*, Pan Books, London.

Harris, T. (1969), *I'm OK - You're OK*, Harper Collins, New York.

Hartford, M. E. (1990), 'Career Education for the Preparation of Practitioners in Gerontology, with special reference to Adult Educators', Sherron, R. and Lumsden, D.B. (eds.), *Introduction to Educational Gerontology* (3rd edition), pp. 187-200, Hemisphere Publishing Corporation, New York.

Hayes, C.L. and Deren, J. M. (eds.) (1990), *Pre-retirement Planning for Women, Program Research and Design*, Springer Publishing Company, New York.

Hayes, J. & Hopson, B.(eds.) (1976), *Transition: Understanding and Managing Personal Change*, Martin Robertson, London.

Heller, A. (1983), *Everyday life*, Routledge and Kegan Paul, London.

Hepworth, M. (1991), 'Positive Ageing and The Mask of Age', *Journal of*

Educational Gerontology, Vol. 6, No. 2, pp. 93-101.

Heron, J. (1990), *Cosmic Psychology*, Endymion Press, London.

Holstein, M. (1994), 'Changing Concepts, Visionary or Short-Sighted', *Ageing International*, June, pp. 20-2.

Hutton, W. (1995), Lecture given to Royal Society of Arts, October 30, London.

Jacobsen, D. (1976), 'Rejection of the Retiree Role: a study of female industrial workers in their 50s', *Human Relations*, Vol. 27, No. 5.

Jackins, D. H. (1981), *The human side of human beings: the theory of re-evaluation counselling*, Rational Land Publishing, Seattle.

Jarvis, P. (1989), 'Retirement: an incomplete ritual', *Educational Gerontology*, Vol. 4, No. 2, pp. 79-84.

Jarvis, P. (1990), 'Trends in Education and Gerontology', *Educational Gerontology*, Vol. 16, No. 4, pp. 401-09.

Jarvis, P. (1992), *Paradoxes of Learning*, Jossey Bass, San Francisco.

Jarvis, P. and Walters, N. (1993), *Adult Education and Theory and Interpretation*, Krieger Publishing Co, Florida.

Johnson, M. L. (1995), 'Lessons from the Open University: Third Age Learning', *Educational Gerontology*, Vol. 21, pp. 415-27.

Jones, D. A. and Vetter, N. J. (1984), 'A survey of those who care for the elderly at home, their problems, their needs', *Social Science in Medicine*, Vol. 19, No. 5, pp. 511-14.

Jong, E. (1994), *Fear of Fifty*, Chatto & Windus, London.

Jung, C. G. (1967), *Collected Works*, Routledge and Kegan Paul, London.

Jung, C.G. (1993), *Modern man in search of a soul*, Harcourt Brace Jovanovich, New York.

Kant, I. (1993), *Critique of Pure Reason*, Everyman, Dent, London. (original edition 1781)

Kaufman, S. (1986), *The Ageless Self: Sources of Meaning in Late Life*, The University of Wisconsin Press, Wisconsin.

Kelly, G. (1963), *A Theory of Personality: the psychology of personal constructs*, Norton, London.

Kitwood, T. (1990), 'The Dialectics of Dementia: With Particular Reference to Alzheimer's Disease', *Ageing and Society*, Vol. 10, No. 2, pp. 177-196.

Kitwood, T. (1993), 'Towards a Theory of Dementia Care: the Interpersonal Process', *Ageing and Society*, Vol. 13, No. 1, pp. 51-67.

Kogan, N. (1990), 'Personality and Aging', Birren, J.E. and Schaie, K.W. (eds.) *Handbook of the Psychology of Aging*, pp. 330-43, 3rd edition, Academic Press, London.

Kohli, M. (1986), 'The World We Forgot: a Historical Review of the Life course', Marshall, V.W. (ed.), *Later Life: The Social Psychology of Ageing*, pp. 271-

303, Sage Publications, London.

Kohli, M. and Rein, M. (1991), 'The Changing Balance of Work and Retirement', Kohli et al (eds.), *Time for Retirement: Comparative Studies of Early Exit from the Labour Force*, pp. 1-35, Cambridge University Press, Cambridge.

Kolland, K. (1993), 'Social Determinants and Potentials of Education in Later Life: the case of Austria', *Educational Gerontology*, Vol. 19, No. 6, pp. 535-50.

Laczko, F. and Phillipson, C. (1991a), *Changing Work and Retirement*, Open University Press, Milton Keynes.

Laczko, F. and Phillipson, C. (1991b), 'Great Britain: the Contradictions of Early Exit', Kohli et al (eds.), *Time for Retirement: Comparative Studies of Early Exit from the Labour Force*, pp. 222-51, Cambridge University Press, Cambridge.

Laslett, P. (1989), *A Fresh Map of Life*, Weidenfield and Nicholson, London.

Levine, S. (1991), *Who dies? an investigation of conscious living and conscious dying*, Gateway Books, Bath.

Liddington, J. (1986), 'One adult in four: who cares? Education and Older Adults', Ward, K. and Taylor, R. (eds.), *Adult Education and the Working Class: Education for the Missing Millions*, pp. 133-57, Croom Helm, London.

Lyotard, J-F. (1974), *The Post-Modern Condition: a report on knowledge*, Manchester University Press, Manchester.

McClusky, H.Y. (1974), 'Education for Aging: the scope of the field and perspectives for the future', Grabowski, S.M. and Mason, D. W. (eds.), *Learning for Aging*, Adult Education Association, Washington DC.

Manheimer, R. and Snodgrass, D. (1993), 'New Roles and Norms for Older Adults through Higher Education', *Educational Gerontology*, Vol. 19, No. 7, pp. 585-95.

Marshall, V. W. (1993), *Social Models of Aging*, symposium paper given to International Gerontological Association meeting, Budapest July 1993, published by Centre for Studies of Ageing, University of Toronto.

Maslow, A. H. (1968), *Towards a Psychology of Being*, Van Nostrand, New York.

Midwinter, E. (1984), *Mutual Aid Universities*, Croom Helm, London.

Midwinter, E. (1991), *The British Gas Report on Attitudes to Ageing*, British Gas, London.

Migliaccio, J. and Corbett, C. (1994), 'Pre and Post Retirement Services', *Human Resources Management and Development Handbook*, pp. 787-801, Tracey, W. R. (ed.) American Management Association, New York.

Moody, H. R. (1976), 'Philosophical Pre-suppositions of Education for Old Age', *Educational Gerontology*, Vol. 1, No. 1, pp. 1-16.

Moody, H. R. (1987) 'Introduction', *Generations*, Vol. 12, No. 2, pp. 5-10.

Moody, H. R. (1993), 'Age, Productivity and Transcendence', Bass, S.A., Caro,

F.G. and Chen, Y-P. (eds.), *Achieving a Productive Aging Society*, pp. 27-40, Greenwood Publishing Group, Inc., Westport, Connecticut.

MORI Survey (1993) commissioned by National Institute for Adult and Continuing Education, Leicester

Morris, B. (1991), *Western Concepts of the Individual*, Berg, Oxford.

Morris, R. (1993), 'Conclusion: Defining the place of the elderly in the twenty-first century', Bass, S.A., Caro, F.G. and Chen, Y-P. (eds.), *Achieving a Productive Aging Society*, pp. 287-93, Greenwood Publishing Company, Westport, Connecticut.

Older Students Research Group (1982), *Older Students in the Open University*, Open University Regional Academic Services, Milton Keynes.

Older Students Research Group (1984), *Older Students in the Open University*, Open University Regional Academic Services, Milton Keynes.

Older Students Research Group (1987), *Older Students in Adult Education*, Open University Regional Academic Services, Milton Keynes.

Parker, S. R. (1980), *Older Workers and Retirement*, HMSO, London.

Parker, S. R. (1982), *Work and Retirement*, Allen and Unwin, London.

Parker, S. R. (1987), 'Retirement in Britain', Markides, K. S. and Cooper, C. L. (eds.), *Retirement in Industrialized Societies*, pp. 77-80, John Wiley and Sons Ltd, Chichester.

Peterson, D.A. (1976), 'Educational Gerontology: the state of the art', *Educational Gerontology*, Vol. 1, No. 1, pp. 61-73.

Peterson, D.A. (1980), 'Who are the educational gerontologists?', *Educational Gerontology*, Vol. 5, No. 1, pp. 65-77.

Peterson, D. A. (1983), *Facilitating Education for Older Learners*, Jossey-Bass Inc., San Francisco, CA.

Peterson, D.A. (1985), Towards a definition of educational gerontology, Sherron, R. and Lumsden, B. (eds.), *Introduction to Educational Gerontology* (2nd edit.), pp. 185-204, Hemisphere Publishing Corporation, New York.

Peterson, D.A. (1990), 'A History of the Education of Older Learners', Sherron, R. and Lumsden, D. B. (eds.), *Introduction to Educational Gerontology* (3rd edition), pp. 1-21, Hemisphere Publishing Corporation, New York.

Phillipson, C. (1982), *Capitalism and the Construction of Old Age*, Macmillan, London.

Phillipson, C. (1987), The Transition to Retirement, Cohen, G. (ed.), *Social Change and the Life Course*, pp. 156-83, Tavistock, London.

Phillipson, C. (1993), 'The Sociology of Retirement', Bond, J., Coleman, P. and Peace, S. (eds.), *Ageing in Society - an introduction to social gerontology* (2nd edition), pp. 180-99, Sage Publications, London.

Phillipson, C. and Strang, P. (1983), *The Impact of Pre-retirement education: a*

149

longitudinal evaluation, University of Keele, Keele, Staffordshire.

Rapid Reports, (1993), *Population and Social Conditions*, Vol. 1, p. 5. Eurostat. Brussels.

Richardson, V. E. (1993), *Retirement Counselling, a handbook for gerontology practitioners*, Springer Publishing Company, New York.

Riker, H.C. and Myers, J.E. (1990), *Retirement Counselling A Practical Guide for Action*, Hemisphere Publishing, New York.

Rogers, C. (1961), *On becoming a person*, Houghton Hofflin, Boston.

Sabat, S. R. and Harré, R. (1992), 'The Construction and Deconstruction of Self in Alzheimer's Disease', *Ageing and Society*, Vol. 12, No. 4, pp. 443-461.

Savishinsky, J. (1995) , 'The unbearable lightness of retirement', *Research on Aging*, Vol. 17, No. 3, pp. 243-59.

Schuller, T. and Walker, A. (1990), *The Time of Our Life - education, employment and retirement in the third age*, Institute for Public Policy Research, London.

Schuller, T. and Bostyn, A. M. (1992), *Learning: Education, training and information in the third age*, Carnegie United Kingdom Trust, Dunfermline.

Scrutton, S. (1989), *Counselling Older People: a creative response to ageing*, Edward Arnold, London.

Seddon, R. (1993), *Understanding the Human Being, Selected writings of Rudolph Steiner*, Rudolph Steiner Press, Bristol.

Selles, R. (1995), *Coping with Uncertainty*, promotional literature of Retirement Life Challenge Ltd., St Albert, Alberta.

Sheppard, H. L. (ed.) (1970), *Toward an Industrial Gerontology*, Schenkman Publishing Co., Cambridge MA.

Sontag, S. (1978), 'The Double Standard of Ageing' reprinted in Carver, V. and Liddiard, P. (eds.), *An Ageing Population*, pp. 72-80, Hodder and Stoughton with Open University Press, Sevenoaks, Kent.

Steiner, C. (1974), *Scripts People Live, Transactional Analysis of Life Scripts*, Bantam Books, New York.

Sugarman, L. (1986), *Lifespan Development*, Open University Press, Milton Keynes.

Swindell, R. and Thompson, J. (1995), 'An international perspective on the University of the Third Age', *Educational Gerontology*, Vol. 21, No. 5, pp. 429-47.

Thompson, P. (1992), '"I Don't Feel Old": Subjective Ageing and the Search for Meaning in Later Life', *Ageing and Society*, Vol. 12, No. 1, pp. 23-47.

Thorndike, E.L. (1931), *Human Learning*, Prentice Hall, New York.

Thornton, J. E. (1992), 'Educational Gerontology in Canada', *Educational Gerontology*, Vol. 18, No. 5, pp. 415-31.

Thorson, J. A. and Waskel, S. A. (1990), ' Educational Gerontology and the

Future', Sherron, R. and Lumsden, D.B. (eds.), *Introduction to Educational Gerontology* (3rd edition), pp. 333-53, Hemisphere Publishing Corporation, New York.

Usher, R. (1989), 'Locating experience in language: towards a poststructuralist theory of experience', *Adult Education Quarterly*, Vol. 40, Part I, pp. 23-32.

Victor, C. (1991), *Health and health care in later life*, Open University Press, Milton Keynes.

Walker, A. (1986), 'Pensions and the Production of Poverty in Old Age', Phillipson, C. and Walker, A. (eds.), *Ageing and Social Policy*, pp. 184-216, Gower, London.

Walker, J. (1992), *Preparing for Retirement: the employer's guide*, Pre-Retirement Association and ACE Books, London.

Webster, A. (1993), Personal communication.

Weil, S.W. and McGill, I. (1989), *Making sense of experiential learning. Diversity in Theory and Practice*, Open University Press, Milton Keynes.

Weiland, S. (1995), 'Critical Gerontology and Education for Older Adults', *Educational Gerontology*, Vol. 21, No. 6, pp. 593-611.

Whycherley, B. (ed) (1994), *Living Skills II*, Outset Publishing, Hastings.

Williams, R. (1990), *A Protestant Legacy: Attitudes to Death and Illness among Older Aberdonians*, Clarendon Press, Oxford.

Winnicott, D.W. (1957), *Collected Papers: through paediatrics to psychoanalysis*, Tavistock, London.

Withnall, A. (1994), 'Setting our own agendas: self-help among older people revisited', *Education and Aging*, Vol. 9, No. 1, pp. 45-56.

Withnall, A. and Percy, K. (1994), *Good Practice in the Education and Training of Older People*, Arena Books, Aldershot.

Woods, R.T. and Brittan, P.G. (1985), *Clinical Psychology and the Elderly*, Croom Helm, London.

Index

negotiation 37-8
National Institute of Adult and
    Continuing Education
    118, 124, 125
non-learning 48
non-retirement 35
older adults learning 47, 57, 60,
    137
old old 95
older learners 49, 51, 58, 123
Older Students Research Group of
    the Open University 57
older workers 6, 14, 17, 21, 124
'outcomes' curriculum model 56
Parker 4, 8
participation 30, 47, 51, 118
patterns of behaviour 61
pedagogy 57
peer learning 52
peer teaching 52
pension(s) 4- 7, 13, 16, 21, 60,
    111-12, 119-20, 136
Pensioners' Convention 138
Pensioners Forums 138
Pensioners' Parliament 138
perceived self 74
personal philosophy 82-4
personality 37, 72, 87
Peterson 23, 30, 31, 40, 50, 57,
    139, 140
Phillipson 5, 6, 18
Phillipson and Strang 28, 82
philosophy 63
political economy 20
portfolio employment 7
positive age-related human resources
    management 124
positive ageing 99
post-modernity 49, 107
post-retirement education 128

poverty 113
Pre-Retirement Association 62, 138
pre-retirement courses 28, 35, 68
pre-retirement education 27, 61,
    66-9, 114, 127-29
pre-retirement educators 27-8, 66
pre-retirement movement 61
pre-retirement preparation 65, 69
preparation for retirement 29, 67
problem-solving 66
productive ageing 4, 13-6, 20,
    24, 119, 120-22
Productive Ageing model 29, 35
productivity 13-4, 119
professional education 126
professional standards 62
protestant work ethic 90
protestantism 119, 131
psychogeriatrics 29
recognition knowledge 53
redemption norm 53
reflection 53
repetition knowledge 53
retirement 3-8, 11, 13, 17-9, 23-6,
    62, 66, 89, 119-20, 131
retirement age 21
retirement education 27-8, 34
review 75
Richardson 128, 130
Riker and Myers 74, 82, 128
risk society 104
rite(s) de passage 29, 31, 36
Rogers 81, 82
role 20
role change(s) 63
role continuity 28
role socialisation 27, 37
role theory 19
Sabat and Harré 98, 99
Schuller and Bostyn 57, 117

0080177

HNK VW

(Ler)

HAROLD BRIDGES LIBRARY
S. MARTIN'S COLLEGE
LANCASTER

re to be returned on or before
t date below.

T 2003

0904181383